GACE School Counseling
Teacher Certification Exam

103
104
603

By: Sharon A. Wynne, M.S.

XAMonline, INC.
Boston

Copyright © 2018 XAMonline, Inc.
All rights reserved. No part of the material protected by this copyright notice may be reproduced or utilized in any form or by any means, electronic or mechanical, including photocopying, recording or by any information storage and retrievable system, without written permission from the copyright holder.

To obtain permission(s) to use the material from this work for any purpose including workshops or seminars, please submit a written request to:

XAMonline, Inc.
21 Orient Avenue
Melrose, MA 02176
Toll Free 1-800-301-4647
Email: info@xamonline.com
Web www.xamonline.com

Library of Congress Cataloging-in-Publication Data
Wynne, Sharon A.

GACE School Counseling 103, 104, 603: Teacher Certification / Sharon A. Wynne.
ISBN 978-1-64239-042-1
1. School Counseling 103, 104, 603   2. Study Guides.   3. GACE
    4. Teachers' Certification & Licensure.   5. Careers

Disclaimer:
The opinions expressed in this publication are the sole works of XAMonline and were created independently from the National Education Association, Educational Testing Service, or any State Department of Education, National Evaluation Systems or other testing affiliates. Between the time of publication and printing, state specific standards as well as testing formats and website information may change that is not included in part or in whole within this product. Sample test questions are developed by XAMonline and reflect similar content as on real tests; however, they are not former tests. XAMonline assembles content that aligns with state standards but makes no claims nor guarantees teacher candidates a passing score. Numerical scores are determined by testing companies such as NES or ETS and then are compared with individual state standards. A passing score varies from state to state.

Printed in the United States of America
GACE: School Counseling 103, 104, 603
ISBN: 978-1-64239-042-1

TEACHER CERTIFICATION STUDY GUIDE

TABLE OF CONTENTS

INDIVIDUAL DEVELOPMENT AND LEARNING 1

Objective 0001   **Understand personal and social development from childhood through adulthood.**

Skill 1.1   Major Theories of Social and Personality Development 1

Skill 1.2   Basic Milestones in Physical, Motor and Language Development 15

Skill 1.3   Special Needs, Individuals and Developmental Variations 16

Objective 0002   **Understand the significance of growth and change in relation to the needs and well-being of students.**

Skill 2.1   The Impact of Stress on School Performance and Students' Well-being 19

Skill 2.2   Child Abuse and Neglect 20

Skill 2.3   Substance Abuse and Addiction 21

Skill 2.4   Suicide, Self-Injury, Eating Disorders and Interpersonal Violence 23

Objective 0003   **Understand the learning process and the academic environment.**

Skill 3.1   Major Theories of Learning and Cognitive Development 26

Skill 3.2   Learning Styles and Individual Differences 28

Objective 0004   **Understand issues and implications of fairness, equity, and diversity in educational, counseling, and guidance contexts.**

Skill 4.1   Creating Positive School Environments 32

Skill 4.2   Bullying, Stereotyping and Prejudice 33

Skill 4.3   Aggression, Violence, and Conflict Resolution 34

EDUCATIONAL EXPLORATION AND CAREER PLANNING 37

Objective 0005 Understand career development theories and life factors related to career decision making.

Skill 5.1 Similarities and Differences of Career Development Theories 37

Skill 5.2 Decision Making and Career Development 41

Objective 0006 Understand the process of education planning in relation to career goals.

Skill 6.1 Evaluating and Identifying Educational and Vocational Materials 44

Skill 6.2 Exploring Education and Career Options 47

Skill 6.3 Locating and Securing Scholarship and Financial Aid Assistance 50

Objective 0007 Understand the development of academic, personal, social, and career skills and their applications in career and education planning.

Skill 7.1 Student Appraisal Data Relevant to Career Development 52

Skill 7.2 Strategies for Developing Employability Skills 54

COUNSELING AND GUIDANCE 57

Objective 0008 Understand principles of counseling, counseling processes, and helping relationships.

Skill 8.1 The Scope of the School Counselor's Role 57

Skill 8.2 Major Counseling Theories and Approaches 58

Skill 8.3 Application of Counseling Theories and Techniques to a Specific Situation 78

Objective 0009 Understand a variety of counseling strategies.

Skill 9.1 Effective Communication Skills 81

Skill 9.2 Resources for Counseling Activities 84

TEACHER CERTIFICATION STUDY GUIDE

Skill 9.3 Communicating Information to Students 85

Skill 9.4 Conducting an Orientation Program to the School and Guidance Program 88

Objective 0010 Understand group dynamics and principles of group counseling.

Skill 10.1 Merits and Limitations of Group Counseling 89

Skill 10.2 Group Dynamics 90

Objective 0011 Understand principles for developing and implementing classroom guidance curricula.

Skill 11.1 Developing Special Programs to Meet Identified Needs 92

Skill 11.2 Basic Prevention Concepts and Other Curricular Strategies 93

CONSULTATION AND COLLABORATION 95

Objective 0012 Understand theories, models, and processes of consultation and strategies for collaborating with teachers and other school personnel.

Skill 12.1 Components of a Consultation Model 95

Skill 12.2 Strategies for Effective Collaboration 98

Objective 0013 Understand strategies for consulting and collaborating with families and community agencies to provide an effective support system for students.

Skill 13.1 Knowledge of Family Dynamics 101

Skill 13.2 Parents and Guardians as Partners 102

Skill 13.3 Referrals to and Use of External Resources 105

Objective 0014 Understand crisis intervention strategies for students, families, schools, and communities facing emergency situations.

Skill 14.1 Core Crisis Intervention Concepts and Approaches 107

Objective 0015   Understand the role of school counselor as advocate.

Skill 15.1   The School Counselor as Advocate 109

ASSESSMENT INSTRUMENTS AND STRATEGIES 110

Objective 0016   Understand characteristics, uses, and limitations of various types of assessment instruments and approaches.

Skill 16.1   Major Functions of Appraisal 110

Skill 16.2   Procedures Involved in Appraisal Administration 112

Objective 0017   Understand measurement and statistical concepts applicable to individual and group assessment in school settings.

Skill 17.1   Knowledge of Measurement Concepts 114

Objective 0018   Understand how to interpret and use assessment to foster individual growth and achievement.

Skill 18.1   Reporting Assessment Results to Students and Parents 116

Skill 18.2   Interpreting Assessment Data 118

PROFESSIONAL IDENTITY AND PRACTICE 120

Objective 0019   Understand how to plan, administer, and evaluate a comprehensive school guidance and counseling program.

Skill 19.1   Components of a Developmental Guidance Program 120

Skill 19.2   Purposes, Types and Basic Steps in Research, Evaluation and Follow-Up 122

Skill 19.3   Needs Assessment and Program Evaluation Techniques 126

Skill 19.4   New Programming: Developing Objectives and Determining Outcomes Based on Data 128

TEACHER CERTIFICATION STUDY GUIDE

Objective 0020   **Understand roles, responsibilities, and professional standards of school counselors.**

Skill 20.1   Professional Standards of the American School Counseling Association (ASCA) and American Counseling Association (ACA) 130

Skill 20.2   Professional Development 132

Objective 0021   **Understand legal and ethical issues related to the rights and responsibilities of students, parents/guardians, and school personnel.**

Skill 21.1   Legal Rights of Students and Parents Concerning Student Records and Assessment Data 134

Skill 21.2   Knowledge of Use of Legislation in Regards to Special Needs Students 135

Skill 21.3   Laws Regarding Child Abuse and Neglect 137

Objective 0022   **Understand applications of current and emerging technology in education and in the professional practice of school counselors.**

Skill 22.1   Using Technology Effectively 142

BIBLIOGRAPHY 143

SAMPLE TEST I 146

SAMPLE TEST II 161

ANSWER KEY 178

RIGOR TABLE 179

SAMPLE TEST I Answer Rationales 180

SAMPLE TEST II Answer Rationales 212

TEACHER CERTIFICATION STUDY GUIDE

Great Study and Testing Tips!

What to study in order to prepare for the subject assessments is the focus of this study guide but equally important is *how* you study.

You can increase your chances of truly mastering the information by taking some simple yet effective steps.

Study Tips:

1. Some foods aid the learning process.

Foods such as milk, nuts, seeds, rice, and oats help your study efforts by releasing natural memory enhancers called CCKs (*cholecystokinin*) composed of *tryptoph*an, *choline* and *phenylalanine*. All of these chemicals enhance the neurotransmitters associated with memory.

Before studying, try a light, protein-rich meal of eggs, turkey or fish. All of these foods release memory-enhancing chemicals. The better the connections in your brain, the more you comprehend. Likewise, before you take a test, stick to a light snack of energy-boosting and relaxing foods. A glass of milk, a piece of fruit, or some peanuts all contain CCKs and help you to relax and focus on the subject at hand.

2. Learn to take great notes.

We learn best when information is organized. When it has a logical structure and we can see relationships between pieces of information helps us assimilate new information.

If your notes are scrawled all over the paper, it fragments the flow of the information. Instead, strive for clarity. Newspapers, for example, use a standard format to achieve clarity. Your notes can be much clearer through use of proper formatting. A very effective format is called the *"Cornell Method."*

> Take a sheet of loose-leaf lined notebook paper and draw a line all the way down the paper about 1-2" from the left-hand edge.
>
> Draw another line across the width of the paper about 1-2" up from the bottom. Repeat this process on the reverse side of the page.

Look at the highly effective result. You have ample room for notes, a left hand margin for special emphasis items or inserting supplementary data from the textbook, a large area at the bottom for a brief summary, and a little rectangular space for just about anything you want.

3. Get the concept and then the details.

Too often we focus on the details and don't grasp an understanding of the concept. However, if you simply memorize only dates, places, or names, you may well miss the whole point of the subject.

A key way to understand things is to put them in your own words. If you are working from a textbook, automatically summarize each paragraph in your mind. If you are outlining text, don't simply copy the author's words.

Rephrase them in your own words. You remember your own thoughts and words much better than someone else's, and will subconsciously tend to associate the important details to the core concepts.

4. Ask why.

Pull apart written material paragraph by paragraph – and don't forget the captions under the illustrations.

If you train your mind to think in a series of questions and answers, not only will you learn more, but you will also have less test anxiety because you are used to answering questions.

Example: If the heading is "Stream Erosion", flip it around to read "Why do streams erode?" Then answer the questions.

5. Read for reinforcement and future needs.

Even if you only have 10 minutes, put your notes or a book in your hand. Your mind is similar to a computer; you have to input data in order to have it processed. *By reading, you are creating the neural connections for future retrieval.* The more times you read something, the more you reinforce the learning of ideas.

Even if you don't fully understand something on the first pass, *your mind stores much of the material for later recall.*

6. Relax to learn: in other words, go into exile.

Our bodies respond to an inner clock called biorhythms. Burning the midnight oil works well for some people, but not others.

If possible, set aside a particular place to study that is free of distractions. Shut off the television, cell phone and pager, and exile your friends and family during your study period.

If you really are bothered by silence, try background music. Light classical music at a low volume has been shown to aid in concentration over other types of music. Music that evokes pleasant emotions without lyrics is highly suggested. Try just about anything by Mozart. It can relax you.

7. Use arrows not highlighters.

At best, it's difficult to read a page full of yellow, pink, blue, and green streaks. Try staring at a neon sign for a while and you'll soon see that the horde of colors obscures the message.

A quick note, a brief dash of color, an underline or an arrow pointing to a particular passage is much clearer than a cascade of highlighted words.

8. Budget your study time.

Although you shouldn't ignore any of the material, *allocate your available study time in the same ratio that topics may appear on the test.* In other words, focus on the areas that are most likely to be included in the test.

Testing Tips:

1. Get smart by playing dumb. Don't read anything into the question.

Don't make an assumption that the test writer is looking for something other than what is asked. Stick to the question as written and don't read anything into it.

2. Read the question and all the choices *twice* before answering the question.

You may miss something by not carefully reading, and then re-reading both the question and the answers.

If you really don't have a clue as to the right answer, leave it blank on the first time through. Go on to the other questions, as they may provide a clue as to how to answer the skipped questions.

TEACHER CERTIFICATION STUDY GUIDE

If later on, you still can't answer the skipped ones . . . **Guess.** The only penalty for guessing is that you *might* get it wrong. One thing is certain; if you don't put anything down, you will get it wrong!

3. Turn the question into a statement.

Look at the way the questions are worded. The syntax of the question usually provides a clue. Does it seem more familiar as a statement rather than as a question? Does it sound strange?

By turning a question into a statement, you may be able to spot if an answer sounds right, and it may also trigger memories of material you have read.

4. Look for hidden clues.

It's actually very difficult to compose multiple-foil (choice) questions without giving away part of the answer in the options presented.

In most multiple-choice questions, you can often readily eliminate one or two of the potential answers. This leaves you with only two real possibilities and automatically your odds go to fifty-fifty with very little work.

5. Trust your instincts.

For every fact you have read, you subconsciously retain something of that knowledge. On questions that you aren't really certain about, go with your basic instincts. **Your first impression on how to answer a question is usually correct.**

6. Mark your answers directly on the test booklet.

Don't bother trying to fill in the optical scan sheet on the first pass through the test. *Just be very careful not to miss-mark your answers when you eventually transcribe them to the scan sheet.*

7. Watch the clock!

You have a set amount of time to answer the questions. Don't get bogged down trying to answer a single question at the expense of 10 questions you can answer more readily.

INDIVIDUAL DEVELOPMENT AND LEARNING: OBJECTIVES 0001-0004

OBJECTIVE 0001 Understand personal and social development from childhood through adulthood.

SKILL 1.1 Major Theories of Social and Personality Development

There are many theories in the literature of human and personality development as well as in counseling and psychotherapy. The major theories explored in this section are psychoanalytic theory (as created by Freud and developed by his followers) and the related psychodynamic models of Erikson and Adler, and behaviorism. In subsequent sections, we address theories of cognitive development (see Skill 3.1) and other theories of counseling and behavior change such as existential, person-centered, Gestalt, cognitive-behavioral, reality, and solution-focused therapies (see Skill 8.1).

PSYCHOANALYTIC THEORY

The basis of most theories of psychology and counseling evolves from the psychoanalytic theory of **Sigmund Freud**. Other theorists who embraced psychoanalytic theory were Otto Rank, Heinz Hartman, Ernest Jones, Anna Freud, Alfred Adler, Heinz Kohut, Erik Erikson, Carl Jung, Karen Horney, Harry Stack Sullivan, John Bowlby, Margaret Mahler, Jacques Lacan, and Nancy Chodorow. Many broadened Freud's original ideas into different schools; these are often collectively referred to as psychodynamic theory and therapy.

Freud viewed human behavior as primarily the manifestation of biological and instinctive drives, unconscious motivation, and irrational forces. He divided the personality into the following parts:

- the ID, the part of the personality that is blind, demanding, pleasure-seeking and insistent; its function is to lessen tension and to return the psyche to a sense of homoeostasis or status quo;
- the EGO, the part of the personality that is the arbitrator between external reality and internal impulses and experiences; and
- the SUPER EGO, the part of the personality representing moral training whose goal is perfection and "doing the right thing".

He also explored the concept of the unconscious by using techniques of dream analysis, post-hypnotic suggestion, and free association. Anxiety and various ego-defense mechanisms were other components of the personality.

Psychoanalytic therapy aims to reconstruct the personality instead of solving immediate problems, with a focus on the past in order to analyze aspects of the unconscious that are manifested in present behavior. Goals for clients include greater insight into their unconscious psychodynamics, an increased ability to understand the connection between their past and present behaviors, and more psychological awareness.

According to psychoanalytic theory, there are five stages of psychosexual development. These stages are:

1. **Oral** - The mouth is the source of satisfaction - If these oral needs are not met, greediness and acquisitiveness may develop as well as the rejection of others' love, fear of intimate relationships, and mistrust of others.

2. **Anal** - Control of the feces is the source of satisfaction - Negative feelings, including rage, hatred, destructiveness and hostility, are experienced if the need to control one's own bodily functions is not successfully resolved.

3. **Phallic** - The phallus (penis/clitoris) are the source of satisfaction - Penis envy and castration anxiety are associated with this stage of development. Resolution of sexual conflicts and sex-role identity is a critical task at this stage with the Electra and Oedipus complexes resulting from difficulties associated with this stage.

4. **Latency** – This stage has been thought to be a relatively calm period of inward and self-centered preoccupation. If not resolved adequately, narcissistic orientation can occur. The latency period usually occurs between the ages of 5 and 12.

5. **Genital** - This stage is signaled by physical maturity. Preoccupation with the sex organs is possible if not adequately resolved.

Psychopathology results from failing to meet one or more critical developmental tasks or becoming fixated at an early level of development. Neurotic personality development is regarded as an incomplete resolution of one of the stages of psychosexual development. Behavior is determined by unconscious forces, early experiences, and sexual and aggressive impetus.

Projection of the client's feelings upon the therapist is used to facilitate therapy; this is called *transference*. To enhance this process, the therapist tries to remain a "blank slate."

Other techniques used in this therapy include:

1. **Maintaining the Analytic Framework** – The therapist strives to adhere to strict relational rules, including nondisclosure on the part of the therapist/analyst, utilizing psychoanalytic techniques maintaining the contractual agreement for payment of fees, and having sessions regularly and consistently.

2. **Free Association** – This technique encourages the client to say whatever comes to mind in order to reveal the unconscious and give the therapist the opportunity to interpret the unconscious thoughts.

3. **Interpretation** – This is the process of analyzing the material the client reveals from the unconscious via free association and dreams.

4. **Dream Analysis** – This process encourages clients to report and discuss their dreams. The client is then encouraged by the therapist to free associate to various parts of and symbols contained in the dream. The analyst offers interpretations.

5. **Analysis and Interpretation of Resistance** – This technique involves an analysis of the ways the client is resisting the process of change.

6. **Analysis and Interpretation of Transference** – In this approach, the therapist interprets and discusses the significance of the transference process and the therapist-client relationship.

Subsequent developments in psychoanalytic theory that are considered "psychodynamic" are still grounded in key concepts from psychoanalytic theory. These include the role of the unconscious in conscious functioning, the relationship between childhood experiences and adult behavior, a developmental framework of personality, and some of the elements of the therapy process.

However, many of these offshoots are more likely to incorporate ideas about the role of external factors such as other people, the environment, and social norms in the development of personality as well as intervention. These theorists focus upon the ego and its development, as well as the development of the self as an individual.

The goal of these theories is to help the client become more aware of the unconscious, as well as to strengthen the ego system so behavior is based upon reality. Psychodynamic theories include **ego psychology**, **object relations**, **attachment theory**, **psychosocial theory**, **analytical psychology**, and **interpersonal therapy**.

Margaret Mahler was instrumental in developing the object relations theory of psychoanalysis. This theory focuses upon predetermined stages of development in which the child focuses less and less upon self and begins to see the world in relation to others. As development progresses, the child transitions from:

1. **"normal infantile autism"** - where the infant responds to physical stress, does not see a unified self, and considers self and mother as one; to a

2. **"symbiotic relationship"** - with the mother from 1-2 months of age, where the infant is dependent upon the mother and expects emotional congruence with the mother (mother also benefits from the relationship); to a

3. **"separation from this symbiotic relationship"** which occurs as the child gains cognitive awareness of being a separate person around 16-18 months of age; to becoming

4. **"individualized"**, a process that takes place from age 18 months to approximately 3 years of age, and finally; into the

5. **"integration of self"** or maturation as a 3-1/2 – 4 year old.

If a trauma occurs during the separation-individuation phase, borderline and narcissistic personalities often develop; in other words, people often have difficulty with regulating their sense of self and their relationships with others.

More recently, **interpersonal therapy** has emerged from psychoanalytic theories. This time-limited approach also incorporates concepts and structure from cognitive-behavioral therapy and other intervention approaches. It is commonly used with people experiencing depression.

A structural overview of the various concepts and schools of thought in psychoanalytic and psychodynamic theory can be found at en.wikipedia.org/wiki/Psychoanalysis.

Contributions of psychoanalytic theory are:
1. This theory is the basis for all psychological theorizing involved in the explanation of human behavior, because it was the first theory.

2. The approach provides a framework for exploring an individual's history and their relationship to the present by way of the unconscious

3. The concept of resolving resistance to the change process is a key aspect of the success of the therapeutic process.

4. Many of the techniques of the therapy can be applied to other therapeutic Models, including the development of interpersonal therapy.

Limitations of the theory include:

1. For people utilizing traditional psychoanalytic therapy, a prolonged therapist training period is required. Further, work with clients also tends to be long-term.

2. The importance of action to alleviate the problem is not recognized.

3. The basic concepts of the theory are not verifiable by empirical research.

4. The theory is based on neurotic rather than healthy personalities.

5. The theory cannot be used in crisis counseling where immediate solutions are needed.

6. Traditional psychoanalytic theory does not take into account social, cultural, and interpersonal variables, although some of the derivative schools of thought in psychodynamic theory do.

Some of the key vocabulary terms used in psychoanalytic and psychodynamic therapy are:

Abreaction - the emotional reliving of past painful experiences.

Anxiety - the result of repressing threatening thoughts or feelings.

Borderline Personality Disorder - the pathology that develops when an individual fails to adequately develop in the separation-individuation phase, characterized by instability, irritability, self-destruction, impulsive anger, and extreme mood shifts.

Compensation - an ego defense mechanism that helps develop positive traits to make up for individual limitations.

Countertransference - a reaction towards the client by the therapist that can interfere with objectivity. It is generally related to the unmet and sometimes unconscious needs of the therapist.

Denial - the distortion of reality in an attempt to avoid dealing with a particular situation.

Displacement - the tendency to point ones' energy toward another person or object in order to reduce ones' own anxiety.

Ego - the part of the personality that mediates between the unconscious instincts and the environment.

Ego-Defense Mechanism - the unconscious process that operate to protect the individual from threatening and anxiety producing thoughts, feelings, and impulses. Examples include displacement, denial, repression and rationalization.

Ego Psychology – a theory of ego development reflecting different stages of life; formulated by Heinz Hartmann, Erik Erikson and other theorists.

Electra Complex - the unconscious sexual feelings of a daughter toward her father coupled with hostility toward her mother.

Free Association - the technique of permitting the client to say whatever comes to mind without censor.

Fixation - the process of getting stuck at a particular stage of psychosexual development.

Id - the part of the personality that is ruled by the pleasure principle. It is the center of the instincts, which are largely unconscious.

Interpretation - a technique of the therapist to explain a particular event or behavior.

Interjection - an ego defense mechanism where the client takes on behavior learned from another.

Libido - the energy of all life instincts including sexual energy.

Narcissistic Personality Disorder - a personality disorder characterized by extreme self-love, an exaggerated sense of self-importance, and an explosive attitude towards others; these attitudes usually hide a poor self-concept.

Object Relations – the theory that describes the interactional system of self and other; this theory is strongly based in developmental concepts.

Oedipus Complex - the unconscious sexual feelings of a son toward his mother coupled with hostility towards his father.

Projection - the tendency on the part of the client to attribute to others the qualities that are unacceptable in his/her own personality.

Psychic Energy - the drive that propels a person's behavior and psychological functioning.

Rationalization - the method of explaining failures or negative occurrences.

Reaction Formation - an ego defense mechanism where a client strives to hide a socially unacceptable thought or feeling with behavior that is considered appropriate.

Regression - an ego defense mechanism of reverting to a less mature stage of development.

Repression - the unconscious act of pushing unacceptable or painful experiences into the unconscious.

Resistance - the client's unwillingness to share feelings and thoughts, or to make changes, in order for the psychoanalytic process to be successful.

Sublimation - the process of redirecting sexual and other biological energies into socially acceptable and creative avenues.

Super Ego - the part of the personality that determines what is right and wrong and strives to "be good."

Symbiosis - a relationship between two individuals that is advantageous or necessary to both. If an individual does not progress beyond this stage, borderline personality disorder can develop.

Transference - the fostering of emotions originally experienced towards one individual upon another individual not connected with the original experience (usually the therapist).

Working Through - the process of exploring unconscious material, ego defenses, transference, and resistance.

ERIKSON'S PSYCHOSOCIAL THEORY OF HUMAN DEVELOPMENT

Erik Erikson built on Freud's work and developed what is referred to as psychosocial theory. It focuses on developmental tasks in relation to self and others. The eight stages of life articulated in this theory are:

1. **Basic Trust vs. Basic Mistrust** – (Birth to approximately 18 months of age). The infant's needs for nourishment and care are satisfied. The response to these needs must be consistent so the infant develops a sense of trust and attachment to one or two adults. Mistrust results if the infant's needs are not met.

2. **Autonomy vs. Shame and Doubt** – (18 to 30 months of age). The child develops an early sense of independence and a measure of some control over the environment. This independence is manifested by self-feeding, dressing, toileting, etc. In this stage the child needs reassurance and support from the adults around him or her Overprotection should be avoided.

3. **Initiative vs. Guilt** – (2-1/2 to 5 years of age). The child develops an imagination and enjoys play-acting adult roles. The child is also learning to perform adult roles and begins to realize restraints are necessary. A pervasive sense of guilt occurs if the child is not successful in initiating everyday activities and tasks.

4. **Industry vs. Inferiority** – (Elementary and middle school years). The child becomes curious with the need to explore and manipulate the environment around her or him. Competency is reached through accomplishments. The child becomes increasingly aware of interactions with others in the school and neighborhood. If a sense of adequacy is not acquired during this stage, feelings of inferiority occur.

5. **Identity vs. Role Confusion** – (Adolescence). The child is striving for an identity and sense of self-worth. Adolescents seek to formulate their own values, beliefs and style of life. They experiment with different lifestyles. If previous stages have not been resolved satisfactorily, the tasks may reoccur here as developmental problems. Resolving unfinished business is one of the major tasks of adolescence.

6. **Intimacy vs. Isolation** - This struggle occurs during young adulthood. The adult becomes willing to be open about self and to commit to a close personal relationship.

7. **Generativity vs. Stagnation** - Maturity is achieved. The task here is to establish and guide the next generation and come to terms with one's dreams and accomplishments.

8. **Ego-Integrity vs. Despair** - This stage occurs during later life. Despair may be experienced by the elderly if ego-integrity is not obtained. When successful, people have a sense of fulfillment about their lives.

ADLERIAN THEORY

Alfred Adler was originally a follower of Freud. Subsequent Adlerians include **Rudolf Dreikers** and **Harold Mosak**. Rudolf Dreikers was instrumental in applying Adlerian principles to group work. Where Freud explored the psychosexual aspects of personality, Adler concentrated upon the psychosocial aspects of human nature. He believed that people are in control of their lives, thus creating an individual lifestyle at an early age.

Adler called his approach *individual psychology*. In contrast to Freud, Adler felt that consciousness rather than unconsciousness was the core of personality theory. He did not believe in reliving childhood experiences, but instead using these early recollections as clues to understanding the lifestyle of the individual.

Adler emphasized the positive abilities of the individual as influenced by societal forces and the capacity of each to reach optimal development. His theory became the basis for the ensuing humanistic theories that abound today. The main goal is confronting basic mistakes and assumptions the client has made and attempting to redirect them. The focus is on examining the beliefs of the client as expressed by his/her behavior.

Some key concepts in Adler's theory are:

- Childhood experiences are not as crucial in themselves as is the attitude toward these experiences.
- All people have a unique lifestyle, none of which are the same.
- One's lifestyle is set by age 5 and is a reaction to perceived inferiority.
- One's lifestyle is learned from early family interactions.
- Behavior is motivated by social needs and has a goal oriented direction.

For more information about Adlerian psychotherapy, go to ourworld.compuserve.com/homepages/hstein/.

Contributions of Adler's theory are:
1. The theory was a major impetus for the development of other humanistic theories.

2. The theory has influenced cognitive-behavioral theories, family therapies, and general mental health work. Currently, it is impacting emerging theories of culturally competent counseling.

The limitations of the theory are:

1. An inability to validate the vaguely defined concepts with empirical data.

2. The oversimplification of complex human functioning.

3. It is based too heavily on a common sense perspective.

Key terms of Adlerian thought are:

Avoiding traps - the therapist's efforts to avoid reinforcing clients' destructive behavior patterns.

Basic Mistakes - self-defeating beliefs (such as an extreme need for security, unattainable goals and doubting one's worth) which influence the formation of one's personality.

Catching oneself - the process of the client to become more aware of self-destructive behavior, irrational thoughts, and the anticipation of events before they happen.

Convictions - the results of life experiences.

Courage - the ability to take risks.

Encouragement - the process used in therapy to help clients reach realistic goals by using all their resources, recognizing their positive traits and transforming negative traits into positive assets.

Family Constellations - "pictures" of family dynamics and relationships.

Fictional Finalism - the ideal image one sees oneself becoming; one's ultimate goal.

Holism - the viewing of one's personality as a whole.

Immediacy - dealing with the present moment in the counseling process.

Individual Psychology - the uniqueness and unity of the individual.

Individuality - the way we develop our own style of striving for competence.

Inferiority Feelings - the negative feeling one has about oneself. These feelings can be both real and imagined.

Life Tasks - the life work of all humans to attain a satisfying lifestyle.

Lifestyle - the way in which one perceives life and upon which the personality is formed.

Motivational Modification - the therapist's interest in helping clients to want to change their' negative lifestyle goals and challenging their basic negative concepts.

Paradoxical Intention - the technique that is characterized by helping the client invoke exaggerated debilitating thoughts and behaviors, helping the client accept and conquer his/her resistance, thus becoming more aware of his/her behavior and being responsible for the consequences of that behavior.

Phenomenological Orientation - the technique of the therapist that attempts to view the world from the client's point of view.

Priorities - a coping method used to obtain satisfaction in life. By pointing out a client's priorities the therapist hopes to help the client realize the feelings invoked in others and the price the client pays by clinging to these negative priorities.

Private Logic - the central psychological framework of the client; the philosophy upon which one bases one's lifestyle, including basic mistakes and faulty assumptions that often do not conform to reality.

Push-Button - a technique that teaches the client that he/she can control and their thoughts and feelings.

Social Interest - the attitude a client has regarding society; a sense of empathy and identification with the larger community.

Spitting in the Client's Soup - a technique that reduces the usefulness of a client's manipulative behavior. By pointing out the manipulation, the therapist effectively defeats the client's anticipated results of the manipulation.

Striving for Superiority - the desire to become competent and perfect; also known as the "**growth force**".

Task Setting and Commitment - the technique taught to the client to formulate realistic, attainable goals that can be revised if necessary.

BEHAVIORISM

The behavioral theories of psychological development and therapy that developed in the 1950s and 1960s were a radical protest to the psychoanalytic theories that had held sway for many years. The key figures in behaviorism were **Arnold Lazarus**, **Albert Bandura**, **Joseph Wolpe** and **Alan Kazdin**. They built on the work of learning theorists (see Skill 1.2). Contemporary behavior therapy utilizes many concepts, research methods, and treatments to account for and change behavior. In contrast to the psychoanalytic theories, behavior therapies are focused on current behavior as well as methods to change self-destructive behaviors.

Behavior theory describes the principles of learned behavior. The main goal of behavior therapy is to eliminate negative learned behaviors or self-defeating behaviors by having the client learn new, more effective and positive ways of dealing with situations that create behavior problems. The client and the therapist work together to formulate goals. In this process, they detail specific methods to address the client's self-defeating behavior. The client must have a sense of ownership regarding the goals in order to make them work.

The job of the therapist in behavior therapy is to
- make the problem clear,
- verbalize the consequences of the behavior manifested by the client,
- serve as a role model for the client,
- help formulate alternative courses of action with possible consequences,
- advocate behavior change, and provide reinforcement to the client when the behavior changes.

There should be an objective assessment of the results of the therapy. The job of the client is to help the therapist explore the alternatives to the problematic behavior, be open to trying new strategies and be willing to take the risk of trying these new strategies outside the therapeutic session.

Although the goals of the therapy are specific and concrete, and the problems are defined, the procedures and techniques of the therapy are contingent upon the needs of each client. Therefore no set of specific techniques is used, although some methods are used more often than others. Some of these methods are relaxation, systematic desensitization, reinforcement, modeling, assertive training, multimodal therapy and self-management programs. Therapy should focus on behavior change, not on attitude change, and actions are expected to follow verbalization (in other words, practice in real life).

Contributions of behavior theory and therapy are:

1. The techniques are based upon empirical research. Any technique that is not effective empirically is discarded.

2. Treatment is based upon the assessment of individual needs.

3. The therapy is effective in the short-term, yielding results that can be widely applied.

4. The approaches can be used with culturally diverse client populations because of the emphasis on teaching the client about the process and the structure of the therapy.

Some of the limitations of the therapy are:

1. Success depends upon the ability to control environmental factors.

2. In institutional settings, there is a danger of imposing conformity at the expense of individual needs.

3. The therapy does not address philosophical human problems such as values and identity issues.

4. The therapist can, if desired, direct a client towards the goals of the therapist instead of the goals of the client. This may be especially true if the therapist does not agree with the client's value system.

5. Past history is not an important factor in the therapy, therefore the assumption is that past experiences and childhood traumatic events do not play a role in present behaviors.

Key terms in behaviorism are:

Assertive Training - Teaching skills and techniques for dealing with difficult situations in ways that are direct, firm and clear. Assertive training often challenges beliefs that accompany a lack of assertiveness and employs the technique of rehearsal.

Basic ID - an acronym for the seven major areas of personality functioning: **b**ehavior, **a**ffect, **s**ensations, **i**magery, **c**ognition, **i**nterpersonal and **d**rugs/biology. (Lazarus, 1981)

Behavior Rehearsal - a technique of trying out new behavioral approaches that can be used in real life situations.

Coaching - providing clients with general principles of how to make effective behavioral changes.

Cognitive Restructuring - the process of identifying and understanding the impact of negative behavior and thoughts, as well as learning to replace them with more realistic and appropriate actions and beliefs.

Contingency Contracting - the specific delineation of behavior to be performed, changed or discontinued, along with the rewards for the performance of these contractual items, the conditions under which these rewards are to be received, and the time limit involved.

Counterconditioning - the process of retraining problem behaviors and introducing new behaviors.

Feedback - the process of providing the client with verbal responses to behavior changes. The two parts of feedback are encouragement and praise for attempting the behavior change, and specific suggestions for making the behavior change work better.

Modeling - the process of showing new ways to do something. The therapist can help the client do this by role-playing the type of behavior that is desired. Albert Bandura has done much of the work in this area.

Multimodal Therapy - the process the therapist evokes in making an evaluation of the client's level of functioning at the beginning of the therapy, and subsequently adjusting procedures and techniques to the goals of the client. The behavior change is a function of techniques, strategies and modeling. Arnold Lazarus developed this type of therapy.

Negative Reinforcement - when the removal of an aversive stimulus is likely to increase a problem behavior.

Operant Conditioning - a concept from B.F. Skinner (a learning theorist) that says behaviors of an active organism are controlled and controllable, even without actual consequences each time.

Positive Reinforcement - a conditioning technique where an individual receives a desirable result for a positive behavior that subsequently increases the probability of that behavior reoccurring.

Progressive Relaxation - a technique employed to increase the ability of the client to control his/her stress level by gradually having the client relax.

Reinforcement - a specific response to a behavior that increases the probability of that behavior being repeated.

Self-Instructional Training/Management - strategies used to teach coping skills in problem situations such as anxiety, depression, and pain. Realistic goals are set and constantly evaluated. The consistent use of a particular strategy is essential, and support systems are important as are the use of self-reinforcement in order to achieve success.

Self-Monitoring - the process of observing one's behavior patterns and interactions in social situations.

Social Learning Theory - a theory originated by Alfred Bandura. The theory holds that behavior is understood by taking into consideration the social conditions under which learning occurs as well as individual psychological factors.

Systematic Desensitization - the process of teaching a client to become less sensitized to a particular stimulus, thereby reducing anxiety. The techniques consist of relaxation exercises combined with an imagined series of progressively more anxiety-producing situations. It was developed by Joseph Wolpe and is based upon the principles of classical conditioning.

Technical Eclecticism - the process of using different techniques from different therapies to achieve behavior change; the results is; flexibility in the therapeutic process.

SKILL 1.2 Basic Milestones in Physical, Motor and Language Development

The majority of changes in physical and motor growth and the development of language occur prior to five years of age. The primary exception to this is the transition at preadolescence (approximately ages 9-12) into puberty. Hormonal shifts and ongoing physical growth become acute at preadolescence and bring children into adolescence and physical maturity.

Language development in elementary school proceeds primarily in terms of the development of vocabulary and increased sophistication in the use of words and concepts.

The key physical and motor developmental milestones for school-age children and adolescents are noted below.

Ages 6-8:

- Growth slows but remains steady.
- Body proportions change, with legs getting longer.
- Less body fat and more muscle develops, with an increase in overall strength.
- Fine motor skills are enhanced, though muscle coordination is still uneven. This results in the ability to write in cursive in addition to the ability to print.
- Permanent teeth come in, sometimes causing crowding if the mouth has not developed enough.

Ages 9-12:

- Significant body changes as puberty approaches: weight gain, pubic and body hair, increased sweating, oily skin, genital development.
- Some children experience joint pain as a result of growth spurts.
- Girls generally develop sooner: their hips widen, breasts start to emerge, menstruation begins.
- Boys enter preadolescence later and their growth changes last longer.

Ages 13-17:

- Puberty is reached; the adolescent is physically mature.
- Girls reach their adult height by age 17; boys continue to add height into their 20s.

The following websites provide detailed information about developmental milestones and changes: **www.ces.ncsu.edu/depts/fcs/human.html, www.littleab.com/ABcare/develoment.html,** and **www.education.com/reference/ontrack/.**

SKILL 1.3   Special Needs, Individuals and Developmental Variations

Any given child's developmental path is not as tidy and consistent as theory and therefore does not always fit into ordered patterns. This is an important concept when considering theories, stages and developmental milestones. Stage theories and lists of developmental milestones need to be considered markers to guide the observer, not absolute standards within which all children will neatly fit.

The differences in children and their rate of development are influenced by the experiences they have and the environment or culture in which they live. Basic differences in caregiver style and availability, the quality of physical nutrition, and the presence or lack of trauma and violence in the environment all impact children's development. Socioeconomic status, gender, language acquisition, basic cognitive ability and heredity are other factors that influence children's development, behavior and their perspective on the world, as do ethnicity and race.

School counselors and other professionals need to be aware of developmental theories and milestones. Such knowledge provides a background against which they are better able to determine if a child or adolescent is developmentally delayed or needs assistance in reaching his or her full potential. However, the uniqueness of each individual should also be perceived and valued when assessing a particular child's developmental status.

Special Populations

Although every student has special needs because he or she is an individual, there are some students who, by virtue of birth or life circumstance, belong to a group with specific needs. Again, as noted previously, not all children and adolescents who belong to a certain group will necessarily fit a description or profile of group characteristics, because each student is an individual. For example, a particular girl may express a learning style more commonly associated with boys.

However, for the purpose of alerting school counselors to issues their students may face, these factors may be of concern to selected populations.

Migrant worker families:

- Chronic disruption in living circumstances and education, resulting in significant gaps in learning.
- Social isolation.
- Inadequate nutrition and medical care.
- Bias due to stereotyping.
- Stress due to the problems noted above as well as economic hardship.

Immigrant families and those for whom English is a second language:

- Loss of homeland and extended family.
- Difficulties with learning, socialization and peer group acceptance due to language limitations.
- Bias due to stereotyping.
- Post-traumatic stress due to precipitating events that prompted immigration and/or losses associated with relocation.

Homeless families:

- Multiple losses and traumas, and related post-traumatic stress.
- Disruption in living circumstances and education, resulting in significant gaps in learning.
- Inadequate nutrition, sleep and medical care.
- Underlying anxiety due to chaotic and/or unpredictable environment.
- Absenteeism for various reasons.

Families displaced due to catastrophic events (such as hurricanes):

- Multiple losses and traumas, and related post-traumatic stress.
- Disruption in living circumstances and education.
- Lack of social network and extended family support.
- Sudden change in economic circumstances.

Families living in poverty:

- Chronic stress due to economic hardship and challenging life circumstances.
- Inadequate resources for special events at school (field trips, testing, dances, sporting events, etc.).
- Inadequate nutrition and medical care.
- Absenteeism due to the need to attend to pressing family matters.

Gifted and talented students:

- Boredom, which may lead to behavior problems.
- Need for special services and/or creative programming.
- Bias due to stereotyping.

Learning support and special education students:

- Increased need for appropriate attention and support from faculty and staff.
- Specific accommodations during standardized testing situations.
- Need for evaluation, special services and/or creative programming.
- Bias due to stereotyping.

Emotional support students:

- Presence of significant mental health issues.
- Increased need for appropriate attention from faculty and staff, including consultation with other professionals, evaluation, referral, and follow-up.
- Specific accommodations during standardized testing situations.
- Need for special services and/or creative programming.
- Bias due to stereotyping.

Sensory-impaired students:

- Specific accommodations for various classroom activities, as well as during standardized testing situations.
- Increased need for consultation with other professionals, and, at times, need for evaluation, referral, and follow-up.
- Need for special services and/or creative programming.
- Bias due to stereotyping.

TEACHER CERTIFICATION STUDY GUIDE

OBJECTIVE 0002   Understand the significance of growth and change in relation to the needs and well-being of students.

SKILL 2.1   Impact of Stress on School Performance and the Well-Being of Students

Students' academic performance and behavior is impacted not only by the school environment but also by a range of external factors. In the previous section, some of the issues facing students at school as well as in their lives outside the school are noted in our discussion of families in particular circumstances and students with exceptional needs. Substance abuse, mental health and other issues are addressed in this section. These circumstances, characteristics and events can all be considered stressors on students.

Development as Stress

The normal challenges of developmental change can also function as stressors in a child's life. As children grow, experience hormonal shifts, increase their skill base, and gradually shift from a focus on family to peers and then to the larger world, they may experience the stress that often accompanies change. Some children seem to move easily from one stage to another; others feel each developmental shift acutely. Some experience generalized anxiety, revert to earlier levels of functioning for a short time, or become clingy and demanding. They may avoid opportunities for new friends, skill development, or extracurricular activities.

It is important for counselors to have an awareness of the range of reactions to developmental change. These responses can be the primary factor underlying difficulties in peer relationships or academic performance. Considering the role of development in each child's experience is crucial to addressing student needs and concerns effectively.

Impact on School Performance

Stressors can negatively impact academic achievement by making it difficult for the student to focus on learning. When a student is homeless, for example, it may be difficult for him or her to attend in class because of lack of sleep, worry about what is happening with a parent, or concerns about where dinner is coming from and other pressing life issues. Similarly, if a child is being abused at home, he or she may have difficulties with attention and focus.

Some stressors, such as medical conditions, may prevent a child from participating in some school activities or require homebound instruction. While accommodations need to be made for alternative programming, the inability to be "part of the group" still may impair peer relationships and affect skill development and motivation.

Stressors can also have a less direct impact. A challenging home life may make it hard for a student to complete homework assignments or study effectively. Chronic stress and traumatic events also contribute to a lack of self confidence, poor motivation, inadequate social skills, depression, anxiety, and other mental health problems. These difficulties may interfere with a student's ability to participate effectively in the school environment. They can also disrupt the student's efforts to study and do homework.

Individuality and Resiliency

Individuals respond in different ways to the same or similar stressors, and the impact of such stressors needs to be assessed for each student. Mitigating factors include coping skills, personality traits, prior experience with stress and trauma, the degree of social isolation created by the stressful event(s), the quality of attachment to and presence of significant adults in the student's life, and the amount and kind of support the student receives in relation to the stressor.

Resiliency is the ability to thrive in spite of difficult circumstances. Research suggests that several of the most important factors in building resiliency are the presence of a caring, competent adult in the child's life, an attitude of hope and interest in life, and good problem solving skills. Helping students identify or find an important adult upon whom they can rely, teaching problem solving and coping skills, and discussing ways to think about what life brings to us are all good strategies for helping students become more resilient. This, in turn, enhances their well-being as well as their capacity for academic and vocational achievement.

SKILL 2.2   Child Abuse and Neglect

Governmental and nongovernmental sources report that between 12 and 15 children out of every thousand children are abused each year by immediate family members or people living in the home. This does not include abuse and violence perpetrated by others outside the home. Also, these numbers reflect only reported cases of abuse. Abuse or neglect may occur for years before it is investigated; in other cases, abuse continues unchecked. Many children are fearful about reporting abuse for a range of reasons, including the desire to protect one's caregivers and worry about the consequences of reporting.

Given the prevalence of abuse and neglect, it is important the counselor recognizes potential signs of child abuse and neglect. When behavioral indicators are present, counselors should meet with students individually to gather more information about suspected abuse, and to determine who in the child's family or network can be an ally.

The easiest type of abuse to detect is *physical abuse*. Unexplained bruises, bite marks, burns, fractures and other physical indicators suggest that a child has been physically abused. In addition the child can exhibit withdrawal and aggressive behavior, self-destructive behavior, self-injury (such as sticking a pencil into parts of the body or pinching oneself), and avoidance of physical contact with others.

Child neglect is indicated by an unattended need for medical care, reported lack of supervision, dirty unkempt and generally poor hygiene, as well as always being hungry. Common behavioral manifestations are falling asleep inappropriately, stealing food, frequent absences, expressions of hunger and self-destructive behaviors.

For the child who has been *sexually abused* there may be some difficulty in sitting or walking, stained clothing, venereal disease and pain or itching in the genital area. The behavioral manifestations can be quite varied. Overtly sexualized behavior in children under the age of 12 may be an indicator, as can attention problems in school work, self-injury, depression, extremely volatile emotions, suicidal thoughts or gestures, and an inability to control one's behavior in children of all ages.

For the *emotionally abused* child the indicators are eating disorders, sleeping problems, loss of energy and chronic complaints. The behavior manifestations include depression, low self-esteem, lack of self confidence, poor peer relations, and suicidal thoughts or gestures.

The Center for Disease Control has information about child abuse and neglect at www.cdc.gov/ncipc/dvp/CMP/default.htm. Information about child sexual abuse is also available at www.nlm.nih.gov/medlineplus/childsexualabuse.html.

SKILL 2.3   Substance Abuse and Addiction

Many students and families are impacted by chemical addiction. School counselors need to have some basic information about drug and alcohol use and abuse. Many resources are available in the form of books and pamphlets as well as on the internet regarding addiction; local treatment programs and rehabilitation centers are often willing to provide in-service training programs for guidance staff and can also provide free literature.

The job of the school counselor is to recognize the signs of addiction and substance abuse in students and, with the cooperation of the student's parent/guardians, make referrals to the proper agency for treatment. Students may need residential care; other times an outpatient or partial hospital program is adequate. It is the counselor's job to follow-up with the treatment provider, and facilitate the transition of the student back into the school setting as needed.

Some of the indicators of substance abuse in students are:

- An inability to perform at school and home in spite of apparent cognitive capacity and the lack of other interfering factors.
- Excessive sleepiness or irritability.
- Mood swings or seeming personality changes.
- Secretive behavior.
- Sudden change in friends.
- Use of substances in dangerous situations despite the possibility of physical harm, such as driving a motor vehicle or swimming.
- Continued use that results in legal problems such as prosecution for drunken driving, arrests for disturbing the peace and possession of a controlled substance.
- Inability to stop using the controlled substance in spite of social problems such as fights, conflict with family and peers, and poor school performance.

Denial is not uncommon when confronting a student with a substance abuse problem. It may be effective for the school to require the student to attend alcohol and/or drug counseling before returning to school if there has been a breach of school rules and policies by the student. A referral to a professional in the drug abuse field for an evaluation is always an appropriate action when counselors are concerned about the possibility of abuse or addiction.

Parental Substance Abuse

Some students are affected by their parent or guardian's use or abuse of drugs and alcohol; they may or may not be users themselves. Many of the indicators of addiction in the home are similar to other stress indicators, such as poor school performance, anxiety, avoidance of intimacy, depression, guilt and over-responsibility. For more information about students with substance-abusing parents see www.puberty101.com/aacap_alcoholc.shtml and kidshealth.org/teen/your_mind/families/coping_alcoholic.html.

General online resources about substance abuse and addiction include www.drugabuse.gov/parent-teacher.html, www.niaaa.nih.gov/FAQs/General-English/default.htm, and www.adolescent-substance-abuse.com/signs-drug-use.html.

SKILL 2.4 Suicide, Self-Injury, Eating Disorders and Interpersonal Violence

The problems of suicide, anorexia, bulimia, sexual assault, dating violence and self-injury are serious, often long term counseling problems beyond the scope of a school counselor's duties. They may require that the counselor communicate with a range of community agencies and personnel. The school counselor's primary tasks are identification, crisis counseling, parental notification, referral, support, and follow up. It is essential that the counselor utilize the school's protocol in these instances, and report the information to school administration. It may also be appropriate for the school counselor to involve the student assistance team within the school setting.

The American Psychiatric Association notes on their webpage for **teen suicide** that although "...the teen suicide rate has declined by over 25 percent since the early 1990s, suicide is the third leading cause of death among young people ages 15 to 24." (See www.healthyminds.org/multimedia/teensuicide.pdf.)

They go on to detail the following statistics about teen suicide:

- It is estimated that depression increases the risk of a first suicide attempt by at least 14-fold.
- Over half of all kids who suffer from depression will eventually attempt suicide at least once, and more than seven percent will die as a result.
- Four times as many men commit suicide than women, but young women attempt suicide three times more frequently than young men.
- Fifty-three percent of young people who commit suicide abuse substances.
- Firearms are used in a little more than half of all youth suicides."

One of the most common and effective methods school personnel have to recognize the suicidal student is in the writings of that student. Often, an English teacher will come to the counselor with a sample of a student's writing that suggests thoughts and/or plans of suicide. Other times, the counselor may learn that the student is thinking about suicide by comments made directly by the student, or from friends of the student who are concerned.

When such information comes to the attention of the counselor, the counselor should meet as soon as possible with the student. If the student is known to the counselor and a rapport has been built, it is appropriate to speak directly with the student, with the teacher's permission, about the material of concern. Even if the counselor does not already have a relationship with the student, sometimes the counselor must proceed without a prior connection and work at building rapport in the moment.

If confirmation of the suicidal intent is received from the student (and in many cases, even if the student does not confirm suicidal intent), the counselor has a duty to inform the parent/guardian(s), the school administration and the school nurse, that the student is currently at risk. Plans for intervention should be made at the time of this discovery. Do not delay until the next day, or until after a weekend. Once the parent/guardian(s) and/or appropriate professionals are notified, the treatment is in the hands of those who have the skills and authority to deal with the problem.

Self-injury is not uncommon in adolescents and sometimes occurs in middle school students as well. Self-injury is direct harm to the body, such as cutting or burning; it is distinguished from a suicide attempt in that the intent behind the self-injury is *not* connected to a wish to die. Self-injury serves to release tension and help the student manage emotional pain and distress. The counselor may learn about such behavior by direct observation (scars, wounds, bandages) or from the student engaging in self-injury or their friends. Like eating disorders, addressing this issue is a long term problem and requires referral to appropriate mental health professionals. However, school counselors may be in the position of providing support to teen who self-injure as well as offering information and referral.

For more information about self-injury, go to www.healingselfinjury.org/.

Anorexia nervosa, where someone starves him / herself, or its variant, **bulimia**, where the person alternately binges on food and then purges by vomiting or using laxatives, are eating disorders that also arise particularly in adolescence. Again, the counselor may recognize the problem by direct observation and/or reports from the student's friends and peers. Addressing these problems with students can be difficult because the student often truly believes he/she is overweight, or has normal eating patterns.

Eating disorders are often associated with depression and low self-esteem, and, unchecked, can lead to malnutrition, body chemistry imbalance, cessation of the menstrual cycle and other endocrine dysfunctions.

See kidshealth.org/parent/nutrition_fit/nutrition/eating_disorders.html for more information, warning signs, and resources for coping with eating disorders in teens.

Intervening with Students about Self-Injury, Suicide and Eating Disorders

When a counselor learns that a student may have an eating disorder, is self-injuring, or is thought to be at risk for suicide, s/he needs to meet with the student to explore the student's perceptions and concerns. It is also the professional responsibility of the counselor along with the school nurse and other medical school personnel to inform the parent/guardian(s). The parent/guardian needs to be aware of the problem and may also need information, support and encouragement in seeking help for their child from the appropriate medical or mental health professional. The school's student assistance team might also be useful in aiding with referral, support, and follow up.

Interpersonal violence is another common problem among teens. One in three teenagers experiences dating violence (www.acadv.org/dating.html) and a number of teens are also raped or sexually assaulted by either an acquaintance or stranger. The issue of interpersonal physical or sexual violence is likely to be brought to school counselors along with the psychological issues noted above. It is not unusual for the friends of students who are being abused to come to the counselors or teachers. Reports of such situations require the same sensitivity and attention that other serious issues demand, including contact with parent/guardian(s) and appropriate referrals. These cases may also require the involvement of law enforcement personnel.

TEACHER CERTIFICATION STUDY GUIDE

OBJECTIVE 0003 Understand the learning process and the academic environment.

SKILL 3.1   Major Theories of Learning and Cognitive Development

Theories about learning are quite varied. Behaviorism (see Skill 1.1) describes much about how individuals learn, and many of the concepts of behaviorism are central to learning and cognitive development. The theorists in this area of study include the functionalists, the associationists and the cognitive developmentalists. (For an interesting description of various theories and models related to learning, see www.learning-theories.com/.)

The study of consciousness within the context of the environment, instead of studying consciousness as an isolated element, was the main contribution of functionalist theorists **Edward Thorndike**, **B.F. Skinner**, **John G. Watson** and **C.L. Hull** to learning theory. They opposed the introspective techniques of psychoanalytic approaches because it did not explore the relationship with other elements in the person's environment. The functionalists insisted that mental function be studied in relationship to the world surrounding the individual. Many of the ideas in behaviorism developed from this work.

Associationist theorists **Ivan Pavlov** and **William Estes** believed that experience or recall of one object builds upon and causes the recall of other objects related to or associated with that object. This is based on the theories of Aristotle. The key concept is that living organisms' responses to environmental stimuli are governed by the sensory, response, and central nervous systems which consist of innate circuitry and memories of past experiences. The response of organisms is therefore dependent upon associating past memories with present stimuli. This theory applied to learning explains how infants expand their sphere of knowledge.

Cognitive theorists **Jean Piaget**, **Edward Tolman**, **Albert Bandura** and **Donald Norman** assign a prominent role to mental processes. The process of learning depends upon information received and the processing of that information which in turn depends upon mental processes, past experiences or behaviors, and present environmental factors. The person, the environment and behavior are interdependent. Faulty cognitive processes develop from inaccurate perceptions, overgeneralization, or incomplete or erroneous information.

Jean Piaget focused on cognition from a developmental perspective. In his view, development is defined as *the adaptive, orderly, changes experienced by the human organism from birth to death*. The child grows cognitively, socially, physically, and morally, gradually and at different rates. These four different types of growth and development impact on the learning process and the behavior patterns of the child.

Piaget studied how we organize knowledge at different times in our lives. He identified four stages of cognitive development. These are:

1. Sensorimotor Stage - From birth to two years. Development is based upon reflex; information is gained through the senses; the child begins to understand the concept of permanence, and begins to develop *problem solving behavior* through trial and error.

2. Pre-operational Stage - From ages two to seven years. The child starts to develop the ability to share experiences with others, uses symbols and shows rudimentary logical mental operations. The child has yet to develop the concept of *conservation,* the ability to understand that certain properties of an object do not change even though their appearance has changed. The concept of *centration* is the child's logic at this stage. This is the ability to focus on only one aspect of the properties of an object and not being able to understand that an object can have multiple properties without inherently changing. *Reversibility* at this stage is the inability of the child to back up and rethink a problem. The child can only respond to perceived appearances.

3. Concrete Operational Stage - From ages seven to eleven. At this stage the child understands the concepts of conservation, centration, and reversibility; masters the operations of classification, the identification of characteristics and serialization, and is capable of inferences. The child can now respond to inferred reality or facts.

4. Formal Operational Stage - From ages eleven to adult. At this stage the child develops and refines the capability of abstract thinking, can deal with hypothetical situations and exercises higher order thinking such as synthesis and evaluation.

One limitation of Piaget's theory is the fact that he did not consider the effect of culture and the social environment on children's development. **Lev Vygotsky** was one theorist who approached cognitive development from a more social standpoint. He suggested that cognitive development started with social interactions and moved inward.

Current theories of cognitive development focus on the concept that humans develop according to various information processing mechanism that are specific to different areas of learning and growth. This is called domain specificity. These theorists argue that information processing is grounded in evolutionary adaptation. A leading proponent of this approach in relation to language acquisition is **Noam Chomsky**.

SKILL 3.2 Learning Styles and Individual Differences

Human learning is a complex human behavior and the way one learns is as individual and unique as each person. Different styles refer to the *preference* a person may have for learning in a particular way; this approach does not suggest that students can only learn in that way. In fact, exposure to varied learning approaches can be beneficial and growth-enhancing.

Research into learning styles has yielded eighteen different elements that contribute to various learning styles. In an attempt to classify this information, **Dunn** and **Dunn** isolated four different learning styles with varying components. These learning styles take into consideration the varied aspects of the way individuals learn. Further, Dunn and Dunn have developed a learning style inventory that assesses each of these elements.

The four major aspects of learning styles and learning environments are:

Environmental Elements: There are four environment elements that affect the way a student learns. These elements are part of the learning style of the student.

The element of *sound* varies with the learning. Some children can block out sound completely when studying and learning; others require complete silence. Others need only relative quiet and while still others must have a familiar sound, such as music or television, to block out extraneous noises that interrupt their train of thought. Still others can concentrate with or without sound, in silence or noise, or with any sound at all.

Light is also a factor in learning but not as critical as the element of sound. Some students need intensely bright lights in order to be comfortable in reading or writing and consequently become drowsy and lethargic in inadequate light. Some students prefer a subdued light to feel comfortable.

Tolerance to *temperature* varies greatly according to the individual. Concentration alters with the need for warmth or coolness, which can affect the degree of productivity of an individual.

The *design* of the study area is often critical to individual learning styles. Some students need an informal setting such as the floor or an easy chair. Others require a more formal setting such as a table or hard chair in order to concentrate adequately and for others there is no need to take into account the design of the site in which they study.

Emotional Elements: The emotional elements involved in the way a student learns also impacts on the quantity and quality of work produced.

The *motivated* student comes to the task with enthusiasm and excitement, asks questions and goes beyond the requirements of the class to explore further related areas. The *unmotivated* student cannot take in too much at one time, needs short assignments and requires the experience of success to continue to achieve. The unmotivated student will often respond to an individualized program of choices, teaming, or self-evaluation.

The trait of *persistence* is the ability to find the answer to a problem no matter how difficult. Persistent students will use resources or other students for help before asking the teacher for answers. They will not give up but continue to work on a problem until it is solved. Other students, such as those with short attention spans, find it difficult to maintain interest in the subject, daydream, become irritated or disruptive, and do not continue to attempt to solve problems for any period of time. These students need to have rules and objectives set out clearly.

The emotionally mature student shows signs of *responsibility* for the completion of the task at hand without constant supervision. Students who have difficulty learning because of reading problems become easily discouraged and need different methods of receiving material. They may need taped instruction, games, small groups or a structured multi-sensory learning packet. Their different learning styles do not conform to the expected norms.

The student who needs *structure* must have specific rules for the completion of an assignment. These include time limits, restriction of options, and a specific way of responding. Different students need different amounts of structure depending upon the learning style and ability to make decisions. The motivated, responsible and persistent student needs little structure while the unmotivated student with learning problems needs the most structure to achieve success.

Sociological Elements: The ability to learn varies with the student depending upon the atmosphere and individuals involved in the teaching situation. Students can learn from different individuals at different times and in different settings. These settings include learning from *peers, by oneself, in pairs or teams, with an adult or teacher, and in a mixed group*. How students learn sociologically can be determined by allowing them to choose their own method of studying and completing assignments with monitoring by the teacher to check on progress.

Physical Elements: The senses of *seeing, hearing, smelling, feeling* and *touching* are instrumental in the way many individuals learn. Those who learn through *visual* senses can see images in their mind; those who learn through their *auditory* senses learn by listening to sounds; those who learn by the *tactile approach* must be able to touch and feel in order to understand and those who learn through their *kinesthetic* senses need to have actual experiences with the shapes and forms of letters and words. Many students learn from a combination of some or all of the elements discussed.

Other physical elements involved in the process of learning include, the taking of food breaks or *intake, the optimum time of day or night*, and *the ability to move around at will*. Adjustments for these learning styles will produce the ideal atmosphere for learning.

Multiple Intelligences

Another theorist in learning styles is **Howard Gardner**. He has developed the idea of multiple intelligences. He posits that there are eight different kinds of intelligence and that each person is more or less inclined to demonstrate each of these. While this theory has engendered some debate in the field of education, it has opened up an important discussion about how schools can better respond to the diversity of students' learning styles. A multiple intelligence survey is available to assess a student's approach to learning. (For more information, see www.infed.org/thinkers/gardner.htm.)

In addition to the Dunn & Dunn Inventory and Gardner's multiple intelligence test, there are other learning style and personality inventories that can help determine the style or combination of styles suited to individual students. These include the **Schmeck, Ribich, & Ramanaiah Inventory of Learning** Process for information processing preferences, the **Myers-Briggs Type Indicator** for personality preferences, and the **Kolb Learning Style Inventory**. The assessment of a student who is having problems learning might give the teacher direction as to useful methods for motivating and encouraging a particular student to succeed.

Gender Differences and Learning Styles

Recent research and some educational practices have recently focused on differences in the ways girls and boys learn and function in the school environment. There is some indication that, as a group, boys tend to be more competitive and individualistic in their approach to learning, whereas girls are more inclined to work cooperatively with others, are more social, and are more interested in understanding ideas than in assessing facts.

Perhaps the most important thing for school counselors to remember is that gender (or other aspect of social identify such as race and ethnicity, immigration status or social class) is only one variable among a range of variables that contribute to the unique development and capabilities of a given individual. Further, differences within a given group (such as girls or boys) are almost always greater than the differences between two such groups. In other words, there is great variation among any given group of students and a range of individual and social factors contribute to these differences. Paying attention to each student's individual needs is the best approach to facilitating academic success.

See www.maec.org/beyond.html#learn and www.aauw.org/research/genderWars.cfm for more information about gender differences in the school environment.

OBJECTIVE 0004 *Understand issues and implications of fairness, equity, and diversity in educational, counseling, and guidance contexts.*

SKILL 4.1   Creating Positive School Environments

A fundamental task of all schools in addressing diversity issues is creating a positive environment within which all students are respected and can thrive. The school counselor can be instrumental in facilitating the positive school environment. While this task cannot be achieved alone by the school counselor or the guidance department, counselors need to be alert to the ways in which positive school environments can be established, and, in many cases, can be instrumental in effecting healthy changes.

Positive school environments share these qualities:

- Core values of respect, integrity, cooperation and care for one another.

- Adults strive to be caring, competent and "in charge" without abusing their power and authority.

- Clear and direct communication is valued, practiced and taught.

- Student success is measured not only by academic achievement but also by the physical, mental, social and emotional health of students.

- Avoidance of stereotyping and bias while still acknowledging and valuing diversity.

- An attitude of "we are all in this together" rather than an "us vs. them" mentality, including a sense of partnership with parent/guardians and the community.

- Opportunities for students to get to know and work with students who are different from them.

- Refusal to allow sexual and other forms of harassment and bullying.

- Conflict resolution, problem-solving skills and violence prevention programs built into the curriculum.

- Policies and procedures are proactive and preventive in nature, including but not limited to crisis management planning and the creation of a safe school climate.

These qualities should exist across the entire school community. In positive school environments, the values and characteristics described above are present among the student population, among the staff, faculty and administration, and between the students and the adults in the school. Ideally, these qualities are also present at the school board level and in all interactions with parents/guardians and community members.

SKILL 4.2   Bullying, Stereotyping and Prejudice

A lack of respect for diversity is often evidenced by bullying behavior. Increasing, schools are finding they need to take action to address stereotyping, prejudice and bullying among students. A number of factors lead to bullying behavior. Stereotypes and prejudice are major contributors, along with personal characteristics and life experiences of the bullying student. These may include poor social skills, distorted self-perceptions, problems with aggression and impulse control, and previous victimization experiences.

Certain characteristics and personality traits of other individuals may serve as magnets for prejudice and stereotyping. Some of these targets are based on membership in a specific group such as gender, race, ethnicity, religion, physical ability, sexual orientation, and age. Stereotypes abound in our culture regarding these characteristics, and these stereotypes are frequently brought into the school setting and used as the basis for teasing and bullying.

However, such stereotypes are not the only source of bias. Anything that makes a person different in the eyes of the perceiver – anything out of the "norm" – can trigger ridicule, ostracism, hate and violence. Some of these perceptual biases are:

- attractiveness vs. unattractiveness
- thin vs. obese individuals
- effeminate males vs. virile males
- masculine females vs. feminine females
- "in" group vs. "out" group (i.e., cool vs. not-cool)

The presence of difference, in and of itself, is not a problem in the larger world or the school setting. In fact, in a positive school environment, such differences are acknowledged and appreciated. The important issue, however, is the way individuals who are perceived as different are treated, and how that treatment affects the social and emotional well-being of the targeted individuals.

There is evidence to suggest that the self-esteem of a student is directly affected by this type of stereotyping. The stereotyping and its effects can begin as early as the first time a child enters school and may continue throughout the life span.

As a result of excessive teasing or bullying, the targeted individual may:

1. Believes there is something wrong with them and considers him/herself a "loser."
2. Develops emotional problems connected with the perceived inferiority.
3. Manifests a lack of motivation and desire to excel as "It doesn't matter what I do as I never do anything right."
4. Displays personality problems.
5. Begins to feel life isn't worth living and contemplates suicide.
6. Begins to harbor thoughts of violence against the perpetrators of the perceived insult.
7. In extreme cases, carries out an act of self-violence or violence against others.

If not educated to accept differences among people, the perpetrator of the stereotyping, prejudice or other bullying type activities is likely to:

1. Escalate the activity.
2. Enlist others to engage in the activity.
3. Become firm in their beliefs that the targeted individual is undesirable.
4. Feel superior to the targeted individual or groups and justify his/her actions.
5. Become resistant to changing attitudes and incorporate them into a way of life.
6. Resort to violence after justifying the violence in his/her mind.

Programs to combat stereotyping, prejudice and biases should be part of the school curriculum. Although the labeling of entire groups of people is irrational, the school must respond rationally and create programs to address with these issues. Students can be taught to respect the rights of others by programs of cooperation and conflict resolution.

A good website for students as well as teachers and counselors on bullying prevention can be found at **stopbullyingnow.hrsa.gov/index.asp**.

SKILL 4.3 Aggression, Violence, Conflict Resolution and Interpersonal Relations

In 2005, the federal Centers for Disease Control and Prevention did a national survey of high school students' risk behaviors and reported this information in relation to school violence:

• 13.6% reported being in a physical fight on school property in the 12 months preceding the survey.

• 18.2% of male students and 8.8% of female students reported being in a physical fight on school property in the 12 months preceding the survey.

• 29.8% of students reported having property stolen or deliberately damaged on school property.

• 6.0% did not go to school on one or more days in the 30 days preceding the survey because they felt unsafe at school or on their way to or from school.

• 6.5% reported carrying a weapon (gun, knife or club) on school property on one or more days in the 30 days preceding the survey.

• 7.9% reported being threatened or injured with a weapon on school property one or more times in the 12 months preceding the survey."

(Source: www.cdc.gov/ncipc/dvp/YV_DataSheet.pdf)

We are all familiar with the school shootings that occur once in a while. However, the above data reflect the equally troubling and perhaps more relevant facts regarding everyday violence in schools. A major factor contributing to violence in schools is the acceptance of violence as a "normal" reaction to perceived injustices. Media depictions of violence may convey a perception that violent retaliation is "normal" and common. Easy access to guns and other weapons, and the effect of both drug abuse and the way the drug culture permeates the larger culture also may contribute to school violence.

In the school setting, administrators, teachers, counselors and support staff have the responsibility to make the school a safe place for all students. Clear policies that delineate safety and guide behavior are useful in working toward this goal. Policies should articulate appropriate behavior on school property and at school events with regard to the following topics, as well as others:

1. Weapons
2. Homicidal and/or suicidal intent
3. Use of drugs and alcohol
4. Self-harm
5. Sexual harassment
6. Bullying
7. Violent threats

TEACHER CERTIFICATION STUDY GUIDE

However, policies are not enough. Preventing violence and resolving conflicts in interpersonal relations are fundamentally related. Programs of violence prevention must be accompanied by programs of constructive conflict resolution so student can learn methods of positive interactions with others, including those who are different. Not only do these programs help create a safe environment in the schools, but they also teach students the skills to resolve future conflicts in their careers, family, and community as adults. A program of violence prevention and conflict resolution acknowledges that while destructive and violent conflicts may be out of control in our society we can strive to minimize them in any particular school, home or other setting.

The conflict resolution program should:

1. Create an atmosphere of cooperation.
2. Have a component of peer meditation training that teaches negotiation, mediation and arbitration skills to students and teachers.
3. Include units in academic classes on methods of negotiation, mediation and arbitration.

Active violence prevention programs include:

1. The elimination of weapons in school by metal detectors, random locker searches and appropriate personnel to monitor the open school areas.
2. A law enforcement presence on the surrounding property of the school for monitoring and enforcement purposes.
3. Training programs for faculty and staff so they are better able to recognize and intervene before and during violent confrontations.
4. A system for identifying students who are or are at risking of becoming perpetrators of violence and refer them to behavior modification, anger management or other appropriate programs.
5. The creation of a district task force to identify and address the causes of violence in the school district.
6. Effective policies addressing violent behavior and a program that assures student protection if they feel they are in danger.
7. Counseling and/or referral for students traumatized by violence.

Bullying and violence prevention resources are available at **www.cdc.gov/ncipc/dvp/YVP/YVP-data.htm** and **mentalhealth.samhsa.gov/15plus/aboutbullying.asp**.

The National Youth Violence Prevention Resource Center offers resources not only on bullying and violence prevention but also addresses substance abuse and other safety issues for teens at www.safeyouth.org/scripts/topics/school.asp.

EDUCATIONAL EXPLORATION AND CAREER PLANNING:
OBJECTIVES 0005-0007

OBJECTIVE 0005 Understand career development theories and life factors related to career decision making.

SKILL 5.1 Similarities and Differences of Major Career Development Theories

There are five different classifications or methods of approach into which most major career counseling theories fall:

1) trait-factor theories
2) societal circumstances of career choice theory
3) developmental theories
4) personality and vocational choice theories and
5) environmental behavioral influences on career choice theories

The **trait-factor theories** assume there is a direct relationship between an individual's interests and abilities and vocational choices. When these are matched, the individual has found their future vocation. Interest inventories, aptitude tests and the general field of vocational testing have been generated from this theory.

The **societal circumstances of career choice theory** contends that circumstances of society, beyond the control of the individual, is the contributing factor in career choice. In this theory, the only control the individual has is in learning to cope with the environment.

The **developmental or self-concept theory** holds that as an individual grows older self-concept changes along with the view of the reality of his/her vocational choice. The satisfaction derived from the chosen career is based upon the individual's self-concept and the relation of that self-concept to the vocational choice.

The **personality and vocational choice theories** are based upon the concept that people of like personalities choose the same types of vocations. The needs of like personalities are the same and therefore they select the same vocations to satisfy those needs. The research done in this area has studied individuals who are already in a specific field as the norm group; their personalities are compared to those wishing to enter the field.

The **environmental behavior theory** incorporates elements of the societal circumstance and personality theories into a classification system that observes the relationship between the interaction of individuals in the environment and their behavior.

Most theorists in career development borrow from each other in formulating their theories. Some of key concepts of the most enduring theories follow:

1. **Bordin**, **Nachmann**, and **Segal** developed a framework for vocational development using a psychoanalytic theory base. By using the occupations of accounting, social work, and plumbing they attempted to generalize a system that might be used to classify occupations into areas of psychoanalytic dimensions.

2, **Ginzberg**, **Ginzberg**, **Axelrad** and **Herma** developed a theory that vocational choice is divided into three stages. The **fantasy period** is characterized by the lack of reality of the child in vocational choice. It is based on the child's imaginings and interests. The **tentative period** is characterized by a shift from the child's *interests* as they become aware that they have more *capacities* in one area than another. They then begin to consider these abilities in vocational choice. As they become older they begin to consider the *value* or satisfaction they get from some activities over others, and in the final stage they begin to incorporate all these subdivisions into the *transition period and* move into the **realistic period.** This period is divided into the *exploration stage* when all the elements of the tentative period are incorporated, with the added insight of what is feasible for the individual. These results come together in the *crystallization stage* that finally leads to the *stage of specification* where the individual finally makes a choice of a specific occupation. The theory is based on the general concepts of developmental psychology.

3. **Holland**'s theory of vocational personalities and work environments is based upon the individual's adjustment to six occupational environments and the interaction of those environments to the personalities of individuals.

The first of these six **occupational environments/personality types** is described as (1) *realistic*, portrayed by individuals who deal better with things than ideas or people, are oriented towards the present, and value tangible things such as money, power, and status. They avoid dealing with subjectivity and intellectualism, and lack social skills. They are persistent, mature and simple. These people are in the occupations of engineering, technical fields, skilled trades and agriculture.

The (2) *investigative* person thinks, organizes, understands, and copes with problems intellectually. They think themselves as intellectuals and scholars and tend to avoid interpersonal relationships. Their achievement is in academic and scientific areas. They hold less conventional attitudes and are found in occupations related to math and science.

The (3) *social* personality seeks satisfaction in therapeutic situations and is skilled in close interpersonal relations. They are sensitive to the needs of others. They are involved in teaching, understanding others, helping others by using their verbal and social skills for behavior changes, and are optimistic, scholarly and verbally oriented. They are found in the helping occupations.

The (4) *conventional* personality values rules and regulations, has a great deal of self-control, is neat and organized, and needs structure and order. They think of themselves as conforming and orderly. They identify with power and status but do not necessarily aspire to obtain those for themselves. They follow orders well. They are found in accounting, business and clerical vocations.

(5) Enterprising individuals are skilled verbally but use these skills for manipulation and domination and aspire to obtain power and status. They are aggressive, self-confident, verbal and social. Political, leadership and power roles are important to them and they aspire to obtain these roles. They are found in occupations of sales, supervision and leadership.

Finally the (6) *artistic* personality relates with others through artistic expression, dislikes structure, and relies on feelings and imagination. They think of themselves as intuitive, introspective, nonconforming, and independent. They value artistic qualities and are not interested in politics. They relate by the use of their artistic abilities. They are found in the arts, music, literature and creative areas.

The characteristics of the environments the above personalities seek closely resemble their traits and therefore dominate the work environment. It follows then that people seek out the work environments that suit their personalities.

4. **Roe** developed the concept that every individual inherits certain ways of expending their energies. This, combined with childhood experiences, results in a style that manifests itself in vocational choices. She draws on the needs theory of Maslow (webspace.ship.edu/cgboer/maslow.html) as well. The concept of genetic disposition together with needs theory and the influence of childhood experiences and innate style come together to form the basis of vocational choice.

5. **Super**'s theory of vocational behavior is based on the development of a vocational self-concept. This theory emerges from developmental psychology and behavior theory in relation to self-concept. He proposes that people express their self-concepts by entering occupations they perceive to allow self-expression. Individuals behavior in order to enhance their self-concept; different behaviors occur as a result of their present stage of life development. As the individual matures the self-concept becomes stable, but external conditions contribute to how that self-concept is expressed vocationally.

Super explored the developmental life stages of the individual in reference to vocational behavior. These stages are similar to Ginzberg's classifications. They include *crystallization*, *specification*, *implementation*, *stabilization*, and, finally, *consolidation*. The adolescent is in the explorer stage in search of a career direction, the young adult seeks job training and job seeking, and the mature adult finds a vocation and secures a position.

6. **Tiedman** and his colleagues saw career development as a result of the developing self. The components include situational, societal and biological factors. The decision making process involves anticipation, implementation and adjustment. The sequence is characterized by an initial level of disorganized thinking about vocations, followed by clearer thinking and then evaluation of the advantages, disadvantages and values of each vocation. Teidman believes the career decision making process to evolve from the relationship between work and non-work activities.

There are many similarities in the theories of vocational choice:

1. Most of the theories are constructive; they describe the nature of the relationship between the person and vocational choice between two sets of observations.

2. The theories are generally descriptive rather than explanatory.

3. There is a great similarity in their explanations.

4. The research has not been experimental. Rather, these theories sort by groups and predict vocational choice based on characteristics of that group.

5. Most of the theories have roots in personality theory.

6. The theories are generally simple and uncomplicated.

There are also some differences:

1. Each of the theories states a particular set of objectives the individual is trying to accomplish through vocational choice.

2. Some theories have sufficient empirical data to support them and others have little empirical support.

3. There is a difference in when the most significant experiences for career development occur and what the critical sources of influence are.

4. The role of aptitudes is given various degrees of influence on career choice by the different theorists.

5. The role of family influence on career choice is treated with varying degrees of importance.

Generally the similarities among the theories are greater than the differences. They emphasize the same types of critical periods in career development and have their roots in personality theory. The differences lie in the choice of emphasis, the research methods appropriate for use in each theory, and the degree to which the relationship between various events occur.

SKILL 5.2   Decision Making and Career Development

The process of decision making is used in all stages of career development. Although decision making in career development is a continuous process there are critical points that occur in the selection of an entry level job, a change of job or a change in educational plans.

H.B. Gelatt in 1962 advocated "a totally rational approach to making decisions." Since then, he has changed his view of decision making to being flexible, keeping an open mind, and using one's intuition. His definition of decision making is "the process of arranging and rearranging information into a course of action."

The three parts of Gelatt's decision making process are as follows:

1. Obtain the information that forms the basis for making the decision. All information can be biased by the fact that it is ever-changing and slanted by the sender of the information.

2. Arrange and rearrange this information by being flexible and having knowledge of your individual needs.

3. Make a choice. Try to be rational but if the decision seems irrational have a good reason for making that decision.

Tiedman and **O'Hara** have noted that career choices are made by decision making processes that are subjective and depend upon the comprehension and control of the person making the decision. Their model tries to make the individual aware of all the factors involved in making the decision so they can make choices based on knowledge of themselves and of all the external factors involved.

They describe a process of decision making that is divided into two phases. The first is the anticipation phase and the second is the accommodation phase. Each has several steps.

Anticipation Phase

In the *exploration stage* the individual investigates all educational, occupational and personal alternatives. They identify interests and capabilities and consider the relationships among them and the alternatives suggested. The counselor provides support and teaching experiences as to the method of exploration and also provides career information.

In the *crystallization stage* the individual organizes, evaluates, synthesizes and orders the personal information and the alternatives from the exploration stage. Ideas are stabilized and formed as to possible career choices. The counselor helps in the organization, evaluation and synthesis of the information. Free discussion of issues and options continue to take place.

In the *choice stage* the individual makes a choice based upon the information gained in the crystallization stage with the consequences of the choice made as part of the process.

In the *clarification stage* the individual forms and carries out a plan to implement their choice. The counselor continues to supply information, support and feedback about the implementation of the choice.

Accommodation Phase

In the *induction stage,* usually during the first months of the implementation of the choice, individuals come to understand the reality of the choice they have made. They begin to learn what is expected and required of them.

In the *reformation stage* individuals work out the realities of the choices they have made, become more comfortable with those choices and begin to rely less on the support and advice of the counselor.

In the *integration stage* of the decision making process, individuals integrate their identities with those in the choice setting and experience a sense of equilibrium.

Because decision making is a product of personality and values, it is important for the individual to have experiences that contribute to their emotional maturity, self-concept and values. Counselors should be the providers of information and resources about the use of that information so that an intelligent choice can be made. The counselor should also help individuals improve upon and perhaps learn different decision making strategies. Ultimately, once the necessary tools and resources are obtained, the decision is the responsibility of the individual.

OBJECTIVE 0006 *Understand the process of education planning in relation to career goals.*

SKILL 6.1 Evaluating and Locating Educational and Career Materials

Appropriate materials are instrumental in helping students make education decisions in relation to their career goals. Finding good materials is part of the school counselor's task. Guidelines for the preparation and evaluation of career and occupational literature have been formulated by the *National Career Development Association* (NCDA). These guidelines are appropriate for use in all vocational and education materials for both publishers and users. They also serve as the basis for ratings of career and occupational literature by the *Career Information Review Service* of NCDA in the *Career Development Quarterly*.

General areas of evaluation should include:

1. *Dates of publication* in order to determine if the material is current. Material over five years old should be discarded as new information is usually available.

2. *Accuracy of information* which is free from distortion and advertising. The material should be reviewed by trained experts in the evaluation process and reflect different points of view. Data should be based upon current and reliable research.

3. The *format* should be clear, concise and interesting.

4. The *vocabulary* should be appropriate to the age and level of the target group. Age ranges should be defined in presenting the material. Material targeted for young high school students, for example, should reflect appropriate language and style. The use of nonsexist language is important.

5. The *purpose of the information* should be presented in the introduction to the material and the target population should be clearly indicated.

6. *Bias and stereotyping* of individuals with a disability, or based upon gender, race, social status, ethnicity, age or religion should be carefully reviewed and deleted. Vocabulary should be gender-free and persons of both sexes should be portrayed equally.

7. The use of *graphics* is valuable but should be presented in a manner that is accurate, current, and unbiased as to sex, race, age and physical disabilities.

The content of all career materials should:

1. Describe the *duties and nature of the work* in a clear and interesting fashion. Literature describing the field should include the importance of the occupation in a global sense; the availability of the occupations; the skills, knowledge and abilities of members in the field; the different levels of occupations in the field; and the nature of any specializations.

2. Portray the *work setting and conditions* of the work environment in terms of the physical and mental duties of the work, the hours, required travel and any aspects of the work that might be considered undesirable.

3. Include the *preparation required* for entrance into the occupation, together with the training, knowledge, skills, and abilities of those successful in the occupation. The levels of preparation in each level of the occupation should also be described.

4. Delineate *special requirements or considerations* needed for employment in the occupation. These include bona fide physical requirements, licensing, and certification or membership requirements. Social and psychological factors that impact on one's lifestyle should also be addressed.

5. Describe a variety of *methods of entry* into the occupation.

6. Include information about *earnings and benefits.*

7. Portray *advancement possibilities* and the criteria for such advancement.

8. Address the long term *employment outlook.* This is an important part of the evaluation.

9. Include *opportunities for experience and exploration* to ascertain if that field is appropriate for a specific individual.

10. Describe *related occupations* that share similar requirements.

11. Offer *additional sources of information.*

The National Career Development Association publishes a Career and Occupational Literature Reviewer's Rating Form that is available from NCDA, 5999 Stevenson Avenue, Alexandria, Va. 20034. This form can be used by guidance departments to rate material that is being considered for purchase for the guidance department or the library.

TEACHER CERTIFICATION STUDY GUIDE

Finding Appropriate Materials

It is the job of the counselor to be able to readily access useful information as needed for different students and varying needs. Becoming familiar with available references can help, followed by regular monitoring of new information. Career and occupational materials change quickly due to frequent shifts in the world of work and technological advances, so the school counselor must stay abreast of current materials.

Federal Government Sources

O*NET, a website run by the U.S. Department of Labor that provides helpful information about career trends to users at no cost. This site can be accessed through the Department of Labor's website for Education and Training Administration at www.doleta.gov/. Other sites and useful documents can be accessed here as well.

This is a list of useful resources from the federal government.

1. Employment & Training Administration, Department of Labor, *Dictionary of Occupational Titles (DOT)* - A comprehensive source of information about occupations and characteristics of the workers in individual occupations.

2. Employment & Training Administration, Department of Labor, *Selected Characteristics of Occupations Defined in the Dictionary of Occupational Titles.*

3. Employment & Training Administration, Department of Labor, *Guide for Occupational Exploration.*

4. Bureau of Labor Statistics, Department of Labor, *Occupational Outlook Handbook.* (Available online at www.bls.gov/oco/; updated every two years.)

5. Bureau of Labor Statistics, Department of Labor, *Occupational Outlook Quarterly.* (Available online at www.bls.gov/opub/ooq/ooqhome.htm.)

6. Department of Defense, *Military Career Guide.*

7. Office of Federal Statistical Policy & Standards, Department of Commerce, *Standard Occupational Classification Manual.*

8. Office of Management & Budget, Executive Office of the President, *Standard Industrial Classification Manual.*

9. National Center for Education Statistics, Department of Education, *A Classification of Industrial Programs.*

TEACHER CERTIFICATION STUDY GUIDE

10. Bureau of the Census, Department of Commerce, *U.S. Census of Population 1990, Classified Index of Industries and Occupations.*

Other Governmental Sources

Regional sources include the *Bureau of Labor Statistics* regional center. Sources from the state of Texas can be obtained through the department of labor at www.twc.state.tx.us/customers/jsemp/jsemp.html and the department of education at www.tea.state.tx.us/. Local sources include the chamber of commerce, the employment and rehabilitative services offices, community colleges and four year institutions, the private industry council, and civic or service organizations.

Commercial Sources of Information

There are many publishers who specialize in providing information about careers and vocations. Always evaluate their products using the guidelines noted above before utilizing these materials. Also be aware of the intent of the source, such as selling a particular product or program.

Skill 6.2   Exploring Career and Education Options

There are many methods of exploring careers and the educational options open to students. They include computer-generated career inventories, career and educational search materials, and detailed information about specific careers and training requirements. The role of the counselor is to help students gather data so they make intelligent, informed and realistic choices. This entails providing information in a timely fashion at the appropriate developmental stage, and following through with support to explore possibilities.

Computer Generated Career Inventories and Search Procedures

Computer assisted advising can very useful to students, counselors and others involved in helping students with educational and career decision. **CHOICES** of Ottawa, Ontario (Canada) is one commercial system that is available to help students explore and research different vocational and career choices. Other career exploration programs include **Discover, Career Information Systems (CIS), Coordinate Occupational Information Network (COIN), Guidance Information System (GIS),** and **Systems of Interactive Guidance and Information (SIGI).**

These programs can give students the ability to hone in on the occupations suited to their personality and fitting with their academic achievement and interests. It is the responsibility of the counselor to become familiar with any network or program, and to teach the student how to access the material. It is also the counselor's responsibility to help the student sift through the data and further explore selected occupations through other means.

Career Day

Community resources are always available to aid the counselor in presenting real life career situations. The organization of the career day program is a time-consuming activity but it offers many opportunities for both the student and the counselor. The counselor makes valuable contacts in the community for future jobs for the students, for creating business relationships to help students and for enhancing the image of the school. Community business institutions are eager to influence young people to enter their professions in order to create a pool of future applicants. The student gathers a wealth of occupational information and can hone in on the areas of most interest. The students can also make their own contacts and make arrangements with businesspeople for further contacts. The counselor should take care to have a representative from each career cluster in order to draw students of varying abilities and interests.

Job Shadowing

Shadowing is the process of spending an extended period of time with a particular person in a field that interests the student as a possible future career. The student does not have to be fully committed to pursuing this career, but should have narrowed down the choices to a few specific careers so to make the best use of everyone's time. The student should be given a set of rules to follow when choosing to participate and a form to fill out for an evaluation of the experience.

The community businessperson should also fill out a form prior to students engaging in job shadowing. Questions such as what the business expects to get from the experience, how much time they are willing to spend with the student and their general practices should be included in the questionnaire. The business should also fill out an evaluation after the student has completed the shadowing experience. A bad experience on the part of the community volunteer might lead that person to not participate in the program the following year, and the counselor needs to know how the process went from the volunteer's perspective.

School-to-Work Programs

One of the best ways to teach students to develop employability skills is to have the student participate in a supervised job experience. Motivation for the student to participate in this type of activity would be to incorporate it into the vocational curriculum and award high school credit to the student for successful completion of this component. Such school-to-work programs can be very useful.

Basic information about effective functioning in the world of work should be conveyed to the student. These include getting to the job on time, avoiding absences for all reasons other than illness, and calling the employer if one is ill and cannot report to work. Many students do not understand the importance of appearance and personal hygiene in obtaining and maintaining a job. These are basics that often have to be taught. In addition, many students have an attitude problem that has been carried over from school. Students need to understand that such attitudes are not tolerated in employment situations.

The instructional component of the school-to-work program should contain extensive material for the evaluation of the student by the employer as to attitude, work habits, personal hygiene, and attendance, as well as knowledge of the job and the ability and willingness to learn and be taught. Weekly work evaluation sheets completed by the employee and the employer show what the student has learned and done well, as well as areas that need improvement. Many school-to-work programs provide these evaluation instruments.

Educational and Vocational Training Opportunities

There are many opportunities for students to obtain work training and education besides the pursuit of a bachelor's degree. Often these other paths lead to higher paying positions in areas that are wide open for employment due to a lack of trained personnel in these areas. Some of these options follow.

1. *Vocational Education* - Often offered by public or regional area vocational centers in daytime, evening and weekend classes. These classes range from basic entry level programs to advanced classes to help students develop a variety of skills in fields such as computers, electricity and plumbing. If a student is of high school age the program is usually part of the high school curriculum. If the individual is of adult age the cost is usually low or there is an opportunity to obtain financial aid. See www.directoryofschools.com/North-American-Trade-Schools/Home.htm for more information.

2. *Community Colleges, Junior Colleges, & Vocational -Technical Colleges -* Most of these schools admit students who might not have the qualifications to enter a four year institution. This gives the student who is a late bloomer or has not done well in high school a second chance. Classes are scheduled so that individuals who may be holding full-time jobs can attend. The cost is usually reasonable and financial aid is available. The completion of these programs can lead to an associate degree, a certificate, a job promotion, or a new career.

3. *Private Career/Proprietary Schools* - These for-profit schools offer training in specific skill areas. They usually are more expensive than a public institution but have placement facilities. Financial aid is usually available. They are accredited by state and/or national groups. A guide to choosing a private career school is Myers and Scott's *Getting Skilled, Getting Ahead.*

4. *Apprenticeship Programs* - These are usually administered through a labor-union industrial council. Forty to fifty occupations are represented by classroom instruction and on-the-job training. The programs involve from two to six years. Contacts for apprenticeship programs can usually be made through the state employment office.

5. *On-the-Job Training-* These programs are similar to apprenticeship programs but are of shorter length and are usually part of a job orientation program for new employees.

6. *The Job Training Partnership Act (JTPA)* - This is an adult training or retraining program funded by the government and run by a local private industry council (PIC) in localities where there is a need for employment training in the area.

7. *Health Related Training* - This type of training is usually available at hospitals or hospital-related institutions where there is an opportunity for clinical or field study as part of the formal instruction.

8. *Military Service* - The military services offer training and continued training in fields that can be used after the individual leaves the service. The Reserve Officers' Training Corps (ROTC) program offers students the opportunity to receive up to a full scholarship for four years of study in exchange for an extended time in the military.

SKILL 6.3   Locating and Securing Scholarship and Financial Aid Assistance

The guidance department should have a collection of books and information to help students locate and secure scholarships and financial aid. There are printed guides available, although many students and parent/guardian(s) find using the internet most helpful.

There are many resources online. Although some commercial sites may provide useful information, they may not be the best or most unbiased sources, and some charge a fee. Two free non-commercial sites with good information are www.finaid.org and www.studentaid.ed.gov. Most colleges and technical schools also provide detailed information about financial aid on their individual websites.

Searching for specific scholarships should not be ignored. The class of the student (such as race, gender, or sexual orientation), area of study, membership in certain organizations and other elements can lead to **specialized financial aid** options. An example of a resource in this arena is "The Higher Education Money Book for Women and Minorities" published by Young, Mathews & Cox.

A great resource for counselors is the financial aid workshops offered by many colleges and universities to interested high schools free of charge. It is the counselor's job to organize and advertise the workshop which is provided by college staff members who are experts in financial aid. Sponsoring a **Financial Aid Night** is an excellent way for students and parent/guardian(s) to gain useful information about aid options and build relationships with the counselors. It is also another chance for the school to promote the guidance program.

Local public and college libraries can be good sources of information as well. Further, it is important that the counselor attends workshops explaining the new regulations involving federal money sources such as the *Pell Grant* and other federal funding sources for educational loans.

OBJECTIVE 0007 Understand the development of academic, personal, social, and career skills and their application in career and education planning.

SKILL 7.1   Student Appraisal Data Relevant to Career Development

Career development is a continuing process. It involves the evaluation of assessment results throughout the life span of an individual. Reflecting this concept, career counseling has grown from a trait-factor, counselor-dominated process to a developmental, client-centered process. This approach views assessment as a tool to increase self-awareness at every major transition period of the individual.

Objectives at each level of development enhance the growth of the individual, with one tool being the assessment instrument. The role of assessment in career development counseling has been recognized as important by the National Occupation Information Coordinating Committee (a federal interagency program) by establishing national guidelines for student and adult career development competencies. Go to www.ed.gov/pubs/TeachersGuide/noicc.html for more information and resources.

At the *elementary school* level, a career development objective might be increased self-awareness in relation to the world of work. This would entail the identification of personal interests, abilities, strengths and weaknesses as well as learning to value the benefits of education. Students could describe school activities that might help them be successful on a job as well as identifying academic skills needed in specific occupations of interest to the student.

At the *middle school* level, a career development objective might be to measure student preferences in different areas and their influence on the student's positive self-concept. This would entail that the student describe their personal likes and dislikes and to know of the benefits of education to career opportunities. The student should learn about his/her strengths and weaknesses in school subjects, what requirements and skills are needed for present and future occupations, the importance of academic and occupational skills in the working world, and the relationship of aptitudes and abilities to occupational groups.

At the *high school* level, it is important for the student to understand the relationship between educational success and work requirements, the role a positive self-concept plays in the world of work, and how individual characteristics relate to achieving life goals. At this level the student should be able to describe the relationship between academic and vocational skills to their own personal interests, ability and skills as well as how they can apply their own skills to present and future occupational needs.

Vernon Zunker, with influence from other theorists, has established a model for the use of assessment results in developmental career counseling. He describes four major steps: analyzing needs, establishing the purpose of testing, determining the instruments to be used, and utilizing the results in decision making for training and education.

The four steps for using assessment results in career counseling are:

Analyze needs - A needs analysis should be conducted using biographical data, interviews, and educational and work records. The cooperation and participation of the individual in establishing their needs is important for the success of the results. To assist the counselor in identifying needs a *counseling relationship must be established* to help the student articulate his/her needs. The *acceptance and adoption of the student's views* will enhance the relationship as well as help in exploring their views in relation to realistic career goals. The *lifestyle needs* of the individual should be part of the needs assessment in order to relate the world of work to the student's values, recreational requirements, financial needs, family responsibilities and societal obligations. The *specific needs* of the individual for assessment should then be examined. A decision should be made as to the need for an assessment instrument.

Establish the purpose of testing - After the needs analysis is completed the counselor and student should decide the purpose of testing. Testing can be used for diagnosis, prediction and comparison of individuals with a normed group. Testing does not always meet all needs that have been identified. The purpose of testing can be specific, as in predicting success in an education or training program, or more general, as in establishing an overall direction of career exploration. The counselor should explain the purpose of each test to be administered as well as the desired results in relation to the stated needs.

Determine the instruments to be used - Tests to be used for career assessment should measure ability, achievement, career maturity, interests, personality and values. Achievement tests measure academic strengths and weaknesses. Career maturity inventories measure vocational development in reference to self-awareness, planning and decision making abilities. Interest tests compare the individual's interests with reference groups. Personality and value inventories reflect traits that influence behavior. Any of the test results can stimulate interaction between the counselor and the student about the relationship between work satisfaction and the actual work.

Utilize the results - The counselor and the student use the results of the assessments to discuss the unique individual characteristics of the student and their relation to career exploration. The test results are also used to help students view themselves as a whole person. Individual traits and characteristics are used to determine plans for the present and to look into the changing future.

SKILL 7.2 **Strategies for Developing Employability Skills**

Attitude and Motivation

When students succeed in their studies they are eager to continue their education. They are more likely, too, to understand the relationship between the acquisition of education and their future lifestyles. When students do not succeed it is very difficult for them to see the value of education and how it relates to their future. When basic survival is demanding the student's attention, and the student does poorly in school, and the tendency to drop out of school or to engage in illicit profitable activities, such as crime and drug dealing, has a fatal attraction.

Counselors can help students facing these challenges to marshal resources to cope with life, as well as help them learn to defer present wants and needs (and peer pressure) in order to receive enhanced rewards at a later date. Further, these students may need specific support regarding academic achievement such as tutoring or special classes.

Exposure to role models who have escaped from poverty and/or crime is important for some students. Persuading such role models to mentor unmotivated students, and providing satisfying educational opportunities in the school may help students explore their potential more fully. Innovative programs can be found by using the resources of the community, the cooperation of parents and the resources of the school. There is also the availability of grant monies to implement programs for unmotivated students in some settings.

Throughout a student's high school career the opportunity to relate subject matter to career and job opportunities should be included in the curriculum of each subject. Job fairs and other types of exposure to job requirements should be presented to students at every opportunity.

An additional method of motivating students to acquire employable skills is to engage community businesses in making a commitment to employ students who adequately prepare themselves for entrance into the job market of the sponsoring business or industry. Apprenticeships, internships and supervised employment while still in school, as a requirement for graduation in a particular area, will encourage students to acquire the skills needed to go from high school graduation to a job that is waiting for them.

When students have incentives they are more likely to work at acquiring the math, English, science and technical skills required by the employer. They will also work at studying other subject areas in which they are not as interested in order to obtain the requirements needed for graduation. When they are working in satisfying positions, they can then have a concrete opportunity to see the need for future education; they may also be able to get their tuition paid for by their employer.

TEACHER CERTIFICATION STUDY GUIDE

Skill Development

Helping students develop skills in various arenas can also be central to school and subsequent career success. Three important skill areas are delineated here: decision-making, studying, and job-seeking.

Helping Students with Decision Making

For adolescents, decision making can be an overwhelming task. Adolescence is a time of self-definition, and therefore many teenagers are faced with both real and imagined crucial life decisions. They may ask "What if I make the wrong decision and I cannot change the course of my life?"

The school counselor's role is to help students understand the decision making process. This can help the student minimize the impact of any one decision causing irreversible harm to the student's present or future. An example of the need for good decision making skills is evident with regard to post-secondary education: a senior has received multiple offers from colleges and cannot decide on which offer to accept.

The process of decision making can be broken down into the following steps:

1. Define the problem clearly.
2. Formulate goals of ideal, acceptable and unacceptable outcomes.
2. Delineate all the possible options, including the option of making no decision at all.
3. Explore the barriers to all the options.
4. Explore the consequences of eliminating one or more of the options.
5. Narrow the options down to manageable choices.
6. Make an informed decision based upon the manageable choices.

Elementary and middle school counselors may not face the same demands regarding student decision making. However, helping students with decisions regarding elective courses and extracurricular activities, for example, can facilitate better decision making at the high school level.

Teaching Study Skills

Efficient ways of studying have been researched by psychologists. Research has yielded a method of studying that helps students retain information and learn in a more organized manner. The following suggestions are the result of these experiments.

1. Make a schedule and stick to it. Study at a certain time each day.

2. Find a place that is comfortable, suits your individual learning style, and is consistently available and convenient.

SCHOOL COUNSELING

3. Have all the materials needed in one place before starting work so study will not be interrupted.

4. Study every day in order to develop the habit of knowing how to study when it is really needed.

5. Keep an accurate and comprehensible notebook in case you need to refer to it.

6. Keep a careful record of assignments. Use a calendar for due dates of all projects.

7. Use short cut devices for retaining information such as flash cards, self-tests or "cover cards" which succinctly detail the material to be retained. Repeat the material orally.

8. Take good notes that list the main points of the material.

9. After learning the material, continue to study to "over-learn." This helps retain the material for a longer period of time.

10. Review frequently after learning the material for the first time.

Developing Job-Seeking Skills

Helping students develop the skills they need to seek and secure a job is also critical, particularly at the high school level. While some of these skills may be taught directly by the school counselor, collaborative efforts with teachers in English, social sciences and other disciplines may be most productive. These teachers can incorporate skill development opportunities into the curriculum, with input from the guidance department.

Some of the areas that may be included are:

- Resume writing

- Filling out job applications

- How to read the want ads

- How to search online for jobs

- Interviewing skills, including how to dress, how to prepare, and appropriate follow-up after the interview

TEACHER CERTIFICATION STUDY GUIDE

COUNSELING AND GUIDANCE:
OBJECTIVES 0008-0011

Objective 0008   Understand principles of counseling, counseling processes, and helping relationships.

SKILL 8.1   The Scope of the School Counselor's Role

The number of guidance activities that the counselor provides for students can be quite extensive, depending on the expectations of the school administrators, the specific job requirements in a particular school setting, and the interests and temperament of the counselor. Some guidance departments divide up tasks such as coordinating all testing, serving as liaison with military and college recruiters, or being the contact person for the local vocational high school. In other districts, school counselors may function in all areas of guidance, even in more than one school and/or level (i.e., elementary, middle or junior high, and high school).

The major tasks of the school counselor are to be a guide and advisor for students and a conduit of information on various topics. The counselor's role often constitutes a kind of "connective tissue" among students, teachers, parents/guardians, and the administration. This is loosely referred to as "counseling."

The school counselor's role may vary significantly from one school district to the next regarding the nature of personal counseling. Some districts expect the school counselor to provide ongoing counseling in varied formats as well as crisis intervention and referral. Others limit the work of the counselor to very short term work, focused primarily on the identification of problems with subsequent referral to community resources. Each counselor needs clarity from the head of the department and the school administrators about the scope of his or her work.

With the exception of specialized schools or alternative education programs, most counselors in a school setting are not in a position to provide in-depth mental health counseling. The demands on counselors are many, and the school environment cannot provide the kind of intervention and support some students require. Effective short term counseling with referral for mental health evaluations by qualified personnel in the community often best meets the needs of students. Ongoing therapy should be provided by community agency clinicians or private practitioners in the area. Early identification of substance abuse and mental health concerns followed by collaboration with parent/guardian(s) and appropriate outside referrals can be key functions for school counselors.

Educational and career counseling generally fall within the purview of the school counselor's role. Other counseling tasks may involve short-term, target-specific psycho-educational groups such as anger management or interpersonal skill development, as well as crisis and/or grief counseling in the event of a death or other trauma in the school community.

Regardless of the extent of a counselor's work in counseling students, there is general agreement that school counselors should not be in the position of school disciplinarian. While there may be an occasion when the school counselor must "write up" a student for a disciplinary problem, as would any faculty or staff member, disciplinary matters should routinely be handled by someone outside of the guidance department. Counselors need to be able to earn and maintain the trust of students; if students don't feel safe with counselors, they are unlikely to seek help from them, or disclose sensitive information to them. Serving as a disciplinarian can undermine trust and interfere with counseling relationships.

Individual Counseling

In many school settings, short-term individual counseling is the most common form of intervention. This modality can be utilized spontaneously as problems arise. Further, it is not limited by the scheduling confines of group counseling. The counselor can tailor the interventions to the particular student's needs and make the most of each session. Drawing on varied techniques, the school counselor can respond to immediate situations as well as longer term issues in individual counseling, helping the student effect change in his or her life.

Sometimes, a school counselor may engage in short term (one to three sessions) counseling with a student, and then determine that the student needs a more intense level of intervention. At this point, a referral for therapy may be made to a community agency or private practitioner. The school counselor's role then shifts to one of follow-up and support. This role is important and should not be seen as less substantial but rather one of changed focus. The student may continue to rely on the counselor as a touchstone and source of information and reassurance, often allowing the outside therapy to be more productive than it might be otherwise.

SKILL 8.2   Major Counseling Theories and Approaches

In Skill 1.1 we addressed several major human development theories that also include counseling approaches and techniques. The theories detailed below are intended to augment the information in Skill 1.1

COGNITIVE-BEHAVIOR THERAPY

In cognitive-behavior therapy clients explore reasons for their behavior by understanding their thoughts. They are also encouraged to look at the ramifications of their behavior on themselves, others, and the environment in which they live and function.

One of the major approaches in the field of cognitive-behavior therapy is *Rational-Emotive Therapy*, **also referred to as Rational-Emotive Behavior Therapy (REBT). Albert Ellis** founded of Rational-Emotive Therapy and is effectively the grandfather of all cognitive-behavior therapies. He believed that the concepts of insight and awareness into childhood events did not result in the resolution of present emotional dysfunction. He also theorized that the connection between the past and the present was not explored fully in psychoanalytic theories.

The key concept in RET holds that even though emotional malfunction is rooted in childhood disturbances, individuals continue to reinforce their irrational and illogical thinking. Emotional problems are the result of irrational beliefs that need to be challenged in order for the individual to resolve the emotional reaction.

The **A-B-C** approach to personality is the basis of RET therapy: A=activating event, B=belief system, C=consequences. RET stresses action and practice in combating irrational and self-delusional ideas. The thinking and belief systems of the client are considered the basis for all personal problems. RET techniques include directed, time-limited, structured approaches for treating depression, anxiety, and phobic behavior. Further developments of cognitive-behavior theory are Aaron Beck's cognitive theory and Donald Meichenbaum's cognitive-behavior modification theory.

Donald Meichenbaum's cognitive-behavior theory has three phases. Clients are instructed to monitor their own behavior in order to identify negative thoughts and feelings. This is called the conceptual phase. The next phase is rehearsal, where the client creates a new internal system by substituting positive thoughts and feelings. In the application phase, the client applies more effective coping skills to real life situations. Focusing on the client's inner speech is a technique that is used in cognitive-behavior modification theory.

Similarly, **Aaron Beck** emphasized the assumption that clients' conversations with themselves play a major role in their behavior. He theorized that the way people feel and behave is based one the way they view their experiences. The therapy is short-term, active, focused and insightful. Beck's concept of automatic thoughts is the idea that certain events trigger emotional responses. The goal of therapy is for clients to recognize and discard self-defeating thinking and correct erroneous beliefs. It has been applied particularly to the treatment of depression. The techniques used in all cognitive-behavioral therapies are derivative of the above theorists and are tailored to the needs of the client. Any method that works may be used, though there is a bias towards approaches with empirical validation.

Cognitive techniques include disputing irrational beliefs, homework, humor and the changing of language to a more positive approach. *Emotive techniques* include imagery, role-playing and shame attacking procedures. *Behavioral techniques* include operant conditioning, self management and modeling. RET is directive, persuasive and confrontational in contrast to cognitive therapy which emphasizes dialogue to discover misconceptions.

Contributions of *cognitive-behavioral* therapy are:

1. Counseling tends to be brief and outcome-focused.

2. Practice and experimenting with new behaviors is emphasized.

3. The therapy stresses the clients' ability to control his/her experience of the world.

4. It is easily used with clients who are action-oriented and willing to accept responsibility for their difficulties.

5. The therapy can be effectively employed in crisis situations.

Limitations of *cognitive-behavioral* therapy are:

1. The underlying reasons for irrational beliefs is not explored, leaving the client open to incorporate additional different irrational beliefs into their belief system.

2. The dialogue aspect of the therapy does not lend itself to working with clients of low intelligence.

3. There is the danger of the therapist imposing his/her views on the client with the potential for psychological harm.

4. Emotional issues are not explored which may limit the effectiveness of the therapy in the long run.

Some of the key terms of *cognitive-behavioral* theory and therapy are:

A-B-C Model - the construct stating that one's problems do not originate from events but from the beliefs one holds about those events. Changing one's beliefs is the best way to change negative feelings.

Arbitrary Inferences - the distorted view of making conclusions without the basis of supporting and relevant evidence; part of Aaron Beck's cognitive therapy.

Automatic Thoughts - ideas (usually outside one's awareness) triggered by a particular event that lead to emotional reactions.

Cognitive Errors - misconceptions and wrong assumptions on the part of the client.

Cognitive Homework - the process used to help a client learn to deal with anxiety and to challenge irrational thinking.

Cognitive Restructuring - the process of replacing negative thoughts with positive thoughts and beliefs.

Cognitive Therapy - a type of therapy focused on changing negative behavior by changing false thinking and beliefs.

Collaborative Empiricism - a concept from Aaron Beck's cognitive therapy that views the client as capable of making objective interpretations of his/her behavior, along with the collaboration of the therapist.

Coping Skills Program - a set of procedures to help clients deal with stressful situations by changing their thinking.

Disputational Method - a method taught to clients in RET to help them challenge irrational beliefs.

Distortion of Reality - inaccurate thinking causing one to act irrationally, emotionally, and subjectively.

Internal Dialogue/Inner Speech - the process used to recognize irrational thoughts.

Irrational Belief - an unreasonable thought leading to emotional problems.

Labeling and Mislabeling - the distorted view of basing one's identity on imperfections and mistakes made in the past.

Musturbation - the word used by Albert Ellis to describe beliefs grounded in *musts, shoulds, and oughts;* a rigid and absolute way of thinking.

Overgeneralization - the distorted process of forming rigid beliefs based upon a single event and then applying them to subsequent events.

Personalization - the tendency for individuals to relate events to themselves when there is no basis for this connection.

Polarized Thinking - a cognitive error of based on an all-or–nothing framework. There are no gray areas in polarized thinking.

Rationality - a way of thinking that will help us attain our goals.

Role-playing - the process of helping a client work through irrational beliefs by practicing new behaviors.

Selective Abstraction - the distorted view of forming conclusions based on an isolated detail of an event.

Self-Instructional Therapy - the concept that the self-talk an individual indulges in directly relates to the things they do in every day life. The therapy consists of training the client to modify self-talk, a form of cognitive restructuring or cognitive behavior modification developed by Donald Meichenbaum.

Shame-Attacking Exercises - a technique of RET encouraging the individual to do things about which they feel shame without believing they are foolish or without becoming embarrassed

Stress-Inoculation Training - a cognitive-behavior modification technique aimed at giving the client the coping tools to restructure the thoughts that lead to stress, and to rehearse the behavior changes in order to solve the emotional problems caused by stressful situations.

EXISTENTIAL THERAPY

The evolution of existential therapy developed as a reaction to the theories of psychoanalysis and behaviorism. Existential theory differs from the psychodynamic and behavior theories in their fundamental presumptions about the nature of human beings. Psychodynamic theories are based upon a deterministic view of human nature; they see personal freedom controlled by irrational actions, past occurrences, and the unconscious. The behaviorists believe freedom is restricted by societal forces.

Existentialists believe the early theorists did not take into account all aspects of human nature. By concentrating on external objective factors, the psychodynamic theorists and the behaviorists ignored the internal frame of reference and subjective experiences of the individual. Existentialists concern themselves with questions of freedom, responsibility and choice, and the meaning of reaching one's full potential. This philosophical basis suggests people must create their own meaning through their choices in a world that is fundamentally meaningless and lonely; the individual must explore what it means to be fully human.

The assumption is that we are free and therefore responsible for our actions and the results of those actions and choices. We are the "authors of our lives" and are not the victims of circumstances because we have the freedom to change those circumstances. See www.existentialpsychotherapy.net for more information.

Some of the early European existentialists were **Ludwig Binswanger**, **Karl Jaspers**, **Medard Boss** and **Viktor Frankl**. Contemporary figures are **Rollo May** and **Irvin Yalom**. Their work is based upon the work of philosophers Dostoyevsky, Heidegger, Nietzsche, Sartre and Buber.

Viktor Frankl expounded the theory of logotherapy, which literally means "healing through reason" (logic). In developing this approach, Frankl was influenced by the earlier European existentialists. Logotherapy is designed to help people find meaning in life through their experiences.

Irvin Yalom wrote Existential Psychotherapy, a central text in the field of existential psychotherapy. In it, he addresses the core issues that make up the existential theory: isolation, meaninglessness, freedom and death within the context of the therapeutic relationship and process.

Rollo May is responsible for converting the European philosophy of existentialism into American theory and practice. He focuses on the subjective aspects of the therapy and believes that freedom and responsibility go hand in hand, with freedom requiring us to accept responsibility for who we become.

This theory requires an intellectual and philosophical approach on the part of the therapist. Existentialist-based therapy is relationship-oriented, experiential and philosophical. It does not have a set regime of techniques but allows for incorporation of techniques from other therapies. The general approach is to focus upon four major concerns of human existence: freedom, isolation, death and meaninglessness.

The basic goals of existentialist therapy are to help clients become aware they are free to make choices to improve their experience of daily life. Clients are encouraged to see past and future choices, to accept the responsibility of their choices, to recognize the factors that hinder their freedom to choose, and to experience an authentic existence.

There are six concepts to which existential therapists ascribe. They are:

1. **We are capable of self-awareness**. The expansion of this awareness, a basic goal of the therapy, is to increase our perception of the freedom to choose and to act on those choices.

2. **We are free beings and must accept the responsibility of that freedom** to decide our own fate. Although we did not choose to be in this world, how we live here and what we do with our lives are our own choices. Each choice we make creates who we are. Whatever the set of circumstances, it is our attitude that determines how we approach a situation and how we survive it.

3. **In preserving our uniqueness, we know who we are** by our relations and interactions with others. Our awareness of this individuality makes us better able to lead an authentic life style.

4. **The meaning of our lives and existence are always in a state of fluidity** as we continue to create ourselves through our actions. These actions are the result of our own choices and we are not victims of forces beyond our control.

5. **Anxiety is a normal state**. It is part of the human condition, an emotional recognition of one's vulnerability and the responsibility of choosing in an uncertain world without any guarantees. Anxiety is the result of a person's awareness of their aloneness. It is not a sick condition, but rather a growth enhancer to motivate us to change conditions that have become intolerable.

6. **Awareness of death** is a human condition that gives meaning to living. Being aware of our ultimate death is the impetus for us to live our lives to the fullest. Life has meaning because it is not forever. The question is not how long we live, as we all will eventually die, but how we live that life, which creates meaning for our every day existence.

The focus of *existential* therapy is:

1. To confront the reality of being in the world alone and facing the anxiety of this isolation,

2. To understand one's subjective world,

3. To revise the assumptions arising from one's subjectivity, and

4. To make choices that lead to the living of an authentic life.

The approach is not based on curing sickness or solving immediate problems, but on utilizing the inherent knowledge of life experiences to live a fuller and more authentic existence.

Contributions of *existential* theory are:

1. The client-therapist relationship is based upon the humanity of the individual.

2. The theory addresses the major concerns of healthy individuals as they go through life cycles by concentrating on issues important to attaining life satisfaction.

3. The model allows for the inclusion of many other modalities within the larger philosophical framework provided by existential theory. In other words, psychodynamic explorations and cognitive-behavior techniques may be employed as part of the therapy.

The limitations of *existential* theory are:

1. A lack of a systematic procedure

2. The concepts can be difficult to comprehend, and require a particular orientation and effort on the part of the therapist.

3. There is no scientific research done on the model.

4. Lower functioning clients, clients in crisis who need immediate direction, and nonverbal clients may not be able to benefit from a philosophical and intellectual approach to problem solving.

Some of the key terms of *existential* therapy are:

Aloneness - a natural human condition from which we can derive strength to become free. When mastered we will have the ability to stand beside others to lend them support in their own aloneness.

Anxiety - the experience we have when we realize we are not immortal, that we face constant choices in an uncertain world, and when we realize we are fundamentally alone.

Authenticity - the ability to be true to our own ideas of a meaningful existence and to accept responsibility for the conditions of our lives, a result of the choices we have made.

Authorship - the concept that we create our own life situations, problems and destinies.

Awareness - the freedom to choose and act on our choices.

"Bad Faith" - the inauthenticity of not accepting the freedom to take responsibility for our own actions.

Existential Guilt - the result of the feelings we have when we permit others to shape our lives and make our choices.

Existential Neurosis - feelings of despair resulting from a failure to make our own choices.

Existential Vacuum - a condition of emptiness and depression that results from a meaningless lifestyle.

Existentialism - a philosophical movement that stresses individual responsibility for creating one's own ways of behaving, thinking, and feeling.

Freedom - the ability to be responsible for our own destiny and to be accountable for our own actions.

Logotherapy - a branch of existential therapy that challenges clients to search for meaning in life; developed by Viktor Frankl.

Meaninglessness - the fact that there is no inherent meaning in living, and it is up to us to create our own system of meaning.

Phenomenology - a method used in therapy to utilize subjective experiences as a therapeutic focus that is used in many existing theories.

Restricted Existence - the condition of one's functioning with a limited awareness of self and the inability to define the true nature of the problem.

"The Courage to Be" - our ability to live to our fullest, rather than living in within the constraints of what others expect; also, the ability to accept limitations and confront the feelings of emptiness that comes when we are to make new choices.

PERSON - CENTERED THERAPY

The founder of person-centered therapy was **Carl Rogers**. In the early 1940's Rogers created the "nondirective counseling" approach. Later he was involved in advocating for the encounter group movement and was a pioneer in the humanistic approach to counseling. He was opposed to the therapist acting as the expert whose advice dictated what the client needed to do to be well. He felt clients contain the ability to become a more fully functioning "self-actualized" person. Rogers believed all people have a "formative tendency" or inner energy which propels us towards fulfillment and self-actualization.

This theory rests upon the assumption that individuals have internal resources to work toward wholeness and self-actualization if properly supported and encouraged. Person-centered therapists believe clients can move forward constructively on their own. The focus is on understanding the feelings and thoughts expressed by the client from the vantage point of the client's subjective world. The theory emphasizes the personality and attitude of the therapist/facilitator, rather than concentrating on techniques (although the skills of active listening and reflecting are most often used).

This approach is a "way of being rather than a way of doing." Positive attitudes and behaviors on the part of the therapist create a climate of growth that not only reaches the client but which surrounds the client. This helps create an aura of "personal power," or the awareness of one's own feelings, needs and values, that is subsequently sensed by others and facilitates effective functioning.

The therapist's role is to create an atmosphere of empathy, acceptance, warmth and caring an environment of unconditional positive regard. The success of the therapy depends upon the therapist maintaining this climate as the major tool for facilitating positive outcomes for the therapy. In this environment, the client begins to drop defensive attitudes and concentrates more on meaningful goals, leading to positive and appropriate actions. Eventually the client uses the learning acquired in the safe environment of the therapy to apply to relationships outside the therapeutic setting. The focus is on experiencing and perceiving the immediate moment as an opportunity for change

Three characteristics of the therapist lend themselves to creating the atmosphere needed for client self-actualization:

Genuineness - the goal of person-centered therapists is to be aware of their feelings and attitudes, their shortcomings and their humility. They do not hide behind a professional demeanor, but align themselves with the person being counseled.

Unconditional Positive Regard - a positive, nonjudgmental acceptance and caring attitude on the part of the therapist.

Empathic Understanding - the ability to accurately sense the feelings and meanings of the client and to express these feeling and meanings so the client understands the therapist is truly in attuned to the client.

For more information about this approach, literature and training options, contact the Association for the Development of the Person Centered Approach at www.adpca.org.

The contributions of *person-centered* therapy are these:

1. The relevance of the therapist as a person breaks from more traditional forms of therapy and offers a more accessible model for some clients.

2. It is a relationship-centered therapy instead of a technique-centered therapy.

3. While the therapist assumes responsibility for creating an environment that is conducive to the client's success the responsibility for the direction of the therapy lies with the client.

4. The theory concentrates on a person's need to account for his/her inner experiences and has relied upon research to validate the concepts, practices and approach.

5. This theory inherently respects individual differences and therefore is very amenable to culturally competent therapy.

The major limitation of this approach is dependent upon the personal limitations of the therapists themselves. Limitations may include the following:

1. There can be lack of genuine empathy. The therapist may hold stereotypes about certain clients that make it difficult for a therapist to have positive regard, warmth, and acceptance for them.

2. The inability of the therapist to practice appropriate self-disclosure can be a problem. A person-centered approach requires that the therapist have the capacity to self-disclose, but also maintain boundaries. Finding this balance and being truly genuine requires a high degree of self-awareness and self-control on the part of the therapist.

3. Temperamentally, a therapist may not be best suited to the person-centered approach. The therapist may not listen well, or too readily makes assumptions. Further, the therapist may be anxious to solve problems rather than understand the problem to be solved, and have the capacity to allow the process of change to unfold.

4. The therapist may lack the belief that the client can change behavior, thus creating an atmosphere conducive to failure.

5. Person-centered therapy is not effective with people in crises situations who are looking for immediate problem solving strategies.

Some of the key terms of *person-centered* therapy are:

Accurate Empathic Understanding - the therapist's ability to sense the client's inner world (i.e., the client's subjective experience).

Congruence - a state in which self-experiences are accurately represented by self-concept; there is a matching of inner experience with external expressions; also refers to the genuineness of the therapist.

Facilitator - the role the therapist takes in person-centered therapy.

Genuineness - a state of authenticity resulting from self-analysis and a willingness to accept the truth of who one is.

Humanistic Psychology - a movement emphasizing freedom, choice, values, growth, self-actualization, spontaneity, creativity, play, humor and psychological health.

Nondirective Counseling - the type of counseling that assumes the client is the one who knows what is best and should not be in a passive role. This results in the therapist permitting the client to lead the counseling instead of the therapist doing the leading.

Incongruence - the discrepancy between self-concept and ideal self-concept. Incongruence usually results in anxiety, which can serve as a clue to the existence of a problem.

Internal Source of Evaluation - the process of looking to oneself for answers to problems.

Personal Power - the sense of strength that comes from knowing oneself and one's ability to mobilize energy. The therapist's ability to access his/her own personal power facilitates the client's development of personal power, rather than for controlling other people.

Self-Actualization - an inner growth force leading to the development of one's potential and the basis of people being trusted to resolve their own problems in a therapeutic relationship.

Therapeutic Conditions - the necessary conditions of the therapeutic relationship that allow the client to change. These conditions include therapist congruence, unconditional positive regard and accurate empathic understanding.

Unconditional Positive Regard - the acceptance of the client's right to all their feelings without conditions imposed by the therapist.

GESTALT THERAPY

Frederick Perls is considered the founder of Gestalt therapy. **Erving** and **Miriam Polster** were key figures in the development of Perls' concepts. The theory stresses the "here and now" and focuses upon bringing together the parts of the personality that are not integrated into the whole person. It also focuses on the "what and how" of behavior as well as the role unfinished business from the past plays in preventing the individual from adequately functioning in the present. The most frequent cause of unfinished business is resentment. Other sources of unfinished business are avoidance, guilt, anger grief and other feelings that remain unresolved.

Perls' theory includes the following five layers of neurosis:

1. The phony layer: acting as others wish us to act, playing games.
2. The phobic layer: avoiding the confrontation of who we really are.
3. The impasse layer: the sense of deadness or foreboding doom.
4. The implosive layer: fully experiencing our deadness.
5. The explosive layer: the releasing of phony roles to experience a feeling of relief.

Gestalt therapy is, in part, derived from existentialist therapy. Some of the major concepts of the therapy are:

- accepting responsibility for being in the here-and-now
- becoming aware of the present moment (itself a therapeutic process)
- facing the issues of avoidance
- dealing with impasses
- dealing with unfinished business from the past

Clients are expected to be active in their own therapy, to do their own interpreting, and to grow through personal contact. Gestalt therapists emphasize the awareness of personal contact at our boundaries with the world via our senses. This awareness is necessary for growth and change. The client resists contact by a variety of methods such as introjection, projection and retroflection. The goals of the therapy are:

- To challenge the client to develop methods of self-support in order to replace the environmental support system presently in effect

- To become more aware of the "here and now" and the self
- To recognize the parts of the self that have been denied
- To assume ownership and responsibility for this denial.

The focus is not on the techniques of the therapy, but on the therapist as a person and the role of helping the client make his/her own interpretations. The techniques of the therapy are to intensify direct experience in the moment. . Clients role-play and experiment with different scenarios to gain greater awareness of their inner conflicts and to intensify their experiences. In the role-playing aspects of the therapy, the therapist asks the client to play out all the roles experienced in a dream sequence, for example, in order for the client to better understand the dream. An "empty chair" may be placed in front of the client as a device to facilitate the expression of feelings.

More information about Gestalt theory and therapy, including access to key journals in the field, is available www.gestalt.org.

Some of the contributions of *Gestalt* theory are:
1. This approach can de-emphasize the intellectualization of the client's problems and focus on here-and-now experience of interpersonal contact.

2. It lends itself to brief therapy due to the intensity of the experiences of the client.

3. It utilizes dreams and unfinished business from the past in order to understand current problems.

4. The theory can be applied to group counseling, school and classroom problems, and workshop settings as well as individual counseling sessions.

Some limitations of *Gestalt* theory are:

1. It does not give much credence to cognitive factors, nor does it emphasize the importance of empathy and positive regard for the client.

2. It can become a technique-oriented theory with the potential of the therapist misdirecting the course of the therapy for the sake of the techniques.

3. The therapist can slip into autocracy, assuming the role of director rather than facilitator.

4. There is a lack of empirical research to validate the theory.

Some key terms in *Gestalt* therapy are:

Aboutism - the speaking of an incident in the past in contrast to speaking of the same incident in the present.

Avoidance - a technique used by clients to keep from facing unfinished business, from feeling uncomfortable emotions and from having to make changes in their life.

Awareness - the process of exploring one's thinking, feelings and actions.

Blaming Games - a technique used by the client to avoid taking responsibility for his/her growth, to avoid staying in the "now", and to prevent themselves from the pain of experiencing the "here and now".

Boundary Disturbance/Resistance to Contact - a technique practiced by individuals who attempt to control their environment; it can have both negative and positive consequences.

Confluence - the blurring of awareness of the difference between oneself and the environment.

Confrontation - the act of becoming aware of differences between verbal and nonverbal expressions, feelings and actions, and thoughts and actions.

Contact boundary – the interface or point of contact between an individual and the world around him or her, including other people.

Deflection - the process of distraction or inattention, making it difficult to sustain contact.

Dichotomy/Polarity - a split in which a person experiences opposing forces.

Explosive Layer - the mode of releasing the pretenses of phony roles in order to achieve a sense of relief and release.

Here-and-Now Awareness - the ability of the client to realize what s/he is experiencing in the present moment.

Impasse - the point at which we are stuck in a stage of less than full maturation. This may be accompanied by feelings of deadness or impending doom and a wish to avoid threatening feelings.

Implosive Level - the mode in which we allow ourselves to fully experience our deadness or inauthenticity. This leads to the chance to make contact with our genuine self.

Introjection - the acceptance of others' beliefs and standards without analyzing, assimilating and internalizing them.

Modes of Defense - the five layers of neurotic avoidance: the phony, the phobic, the impasse, the implosive and the explosive.

Phobic Layer - the mode of the avoiding of the emotional pain that comes with recognizing our real selves.

Phony Layer - the mode of reacting to others in stereotypical and inauthentic ways, in other words, playing games.

"Play the Projection" - a technique used to help clients see how they project onto others things they do not want to recognize in themselves.

Projection - disowning parts of ourselves by blaming them on the environment.

Resistance - defenses developed which prevent fully experiencing the present.

Retroflection - turning back to ourselves what we would like to do or have done to others.

Unfinished Business - unexpressed feelings (such as resentment, guilt, anger and grief) from childhood that are presently preventing effective psychological functioning; needless emotional garbage.

REALITY THERAPY

William Glasser developed the concept of reality therapy in the 1950s and 1960s. Originally, the approach emphasized individual responsibility. In the 1980s Glasser expanded this concept to a theory of control. Control theory emphasizes doing and thinking. The theory attempts to explain why and how people behave from the point of view of the subjective internal perception of their world. Glasser posits that the purpose of behaving the way we do is to eliminate the discrepancy between what we presently have and what we want.

The theory is also based upon the assertion that we are in charge of our lives, we choose our forms of behavior, and that behavior is intended to increase self-esteem and a sense of belonging, and to attain power and freedom. The therapy focuses on exploring ways to effectively manage our world so we can get what we want without hurting others in the process.

Reality therapy does not dwell on the past, the unconscious, the role of insight, or take into consideration the process of transference. Its goal is to help client clients acquire skills to take control of their lives, better cope with life's demands, and solve present day problems. The purpose is to achieve a satisfying, effective existence. The challenge in therapy is to examine how people are presently functioning in order to improve that functioning. The therapy is short-term and designed to help people develop a "success identity" by meeting the four psychological needs of belonging, power, freedom, and fun.

The therapist's relationship with the client is one of concern, support, and warmth. While the therapist is involved with clients in a positive way, he/she does not accept excuses for inappropriate behavior, and continuously prods and pushes to help the client accept reality and responsibility for his/her actions. The client is expected to take responsibility for deciding what goals to pursue and commit to those goals, to make value judgments about his/her current behavior, to plan a specific course of action for future success, and to make a commitment to carry out these plans in every day life.

The *WDEP model* is the procedure applied in the practice of reality-therapy.

W=Wants - Through questioning by the therapist, clients are able to express their wants, needs and perceptions of what is happening in every day life.

D=Doing - The therapist explores what clients are doing and what direction they are taking in their behavior to obtain those wants and needs.

E=Evaluation - The therapist encourages clients to evaluate their behavior patterns that help or do not help obtain those needs and wants.

P=Planning and Commitment - The therapist invites and encourages clients to plan for behavior change and commit to that change.

Glasser originally used his therapy in working with youthful offenders but the theory of control has been successfully used in individual, marital, family and group counseling, in alcohol and drug abuse clinics, and with students, teachers and administrators.

Contributions of *reality* theory are:

1. Clients are responsible for evaluating and changing their behavior.

2. The client is the catalyst in making specific plans, forming contracts for action and evaluating the success of these actions.

3. The emphasis is upon accountability. No excuses for failure are accepted but blame and punishment for not carrying out the stated changes are avoided. The focus instead is on what prevented the client from carrying out the plan of action and the readjustment to a more reasonable plan of action.

4. There is a structure to evaluate the degree and nature of the changes affected.

5. It is a short-term, clear and easily understood therapy that is applicable to different situations and clients, some of whom may not usually be receptive to other therapy approaches.

Limitations of *reality* therapy are:

1. Consideration is not given to feelings, the unconscious, and the past.

2. The influence of the culture and environment of the client is not taken into consideration when looking for alternatives to the maladjusted behavior. The focus is on the symptoms. The origin of the behavior is not taken into account.

3. There is a lack of research on reality therapy to establish its effectiveness.

Key terms of this approach are:

Autonomy - the acceptance of responsibility and the taking control of the direction of one's life; a state of maturity

Commitment - the ability on the part of the client to continue with a reasonable plan to effect the desired change

Control Theory - a theory of why people act the way they do; the internal motivation to master one's own world.

Involvement - the role of the therapist with the client in reality therapy, a vital part of establishing a relationship with the client.

Paining Behaviors - the manifestation of pain symptoms, such as depression, to refocus the problem on the symptoms instead of the behavior.

Perceived World - one's subjective world.

Picture Album - the perceived reality of the client formulated to meet their psychological needs.

Positive Addiction - the acts performed to gain psychological strength such as physical activity and meditation.

Responsibility - the dependable manner in which we satisfy our needs without interfering with the rights of others.

Success Identity - the state of self-esteem needed to fulfill the behaviors deemed necessary for attaining a more satisfying life experience. The end result of attaining a success identity is that the individual is able to give and receive love, has a sense of self-worth, and possesses the strength to create a satisfying life.

Total Behavior - the blend of the sum of all our activities that forms our personality and the person we have become.

Value Judgment - the evaluation of current behaviors to determine their value.

WDEP System - the abbreviation for the components of reality therapy: the identification of **w**ants, the **d**irection of behavior, the **e**valuation of self, and the **p**lan for change.

SOLUTION-FOCUSED THERAPY

Solution-focused therapy was initially developed by **deShazer** and **Berg** in recent years. The theory is based on work by various family therapists and the work of **Milton Erickson.** It is considered a brief therapy model, sometimes only comprising one session, which lends itself well to many guidance situations.

This model asserts that when clients come to counseling they have a picture of what they would like to be different about their lives and often have the answers to their problems. By providing a constructivist process, the counselor facilitates the process by helping the client in defining the problem, identifying viable solutions, and planning for working towards the desired behavior or reality. The core of solution-focused therapy lies not in the "why" but the "how." Theorists of this orientation argue that the past cannot be changed, so why not focus on how the client wants the future to be more satisfying?

Walter & Peller identified the following guides to making therapeutic choices:

1. Don't bother with what works. Make a determination to do more of it. Success can only be maximized.

2. Build on the small successes.

3. Experimentation is encouraged. Just because something has not been solved in the past it does not mean what was tried is the only possible solution.

4. Change is about the "here and now." Make the most of the current session.

A major focus of the work involves the counselor asking a range of questions to help draw out possible solutions. The solution-focused counselor first asks about the goal the client is hoping to achieve and is not dissuaded or discouraged it the client replies, "I don't know." The counselor empathically reframes these initial questions in order to solicit a goal. Effective goal-setting is critical to the success of solution-focused therapy.

The counselor facilitates the client's desire for change by asking what would be different if, after a night of sleep, the undesired behavior or situation had changed. The client is then engaged in a creative process of constructing a vision of positive behavioral difference or success. The counselor uses the vision as a framework upon which a solution will be defined.

Other questions are used to help the client identify desirable outcomes. The counselor's job is to reflect back the answers in ways that help clients better understand their strengths and skills as well as the nature of the problem. By the end of the session, the counselor assigns the solution as homework to practice in the time between the current and next session. The success of the applied solution can be reviewed in a following session, if there is one.

Contributions of *solution-focused* therapy:

1. Therapeutic work is accomplished with relatively few sessions.

2. Counseling is focused on the reality of the client and is not dependent on the interpretation of the client about past experience.

3. Clients are empowered to make change by what they envision of themselves through magical thinking.

4. The work is solution-focused, not problem-focused.

Limitations of *solution-focused* therapy:

1. Long-term and personality-based issues cannot be resolved by finding a solution.

2. Problems are over-generalized and oversimplified without in-depth consideration to the level of impact on the client's reality.

3. More empirical research needs to be conducted.

Some key terms of *solution-focused* therapy:

Coping questions - a series of questions the counselor uses to help the client identify previously unrecognized coping skills and strengths.

Exception-seeking question – a way to help clients discover the times when the identified problem does NOT trouble them.

Miracle question - a technique wherein the counselor encourages the client to imagine what it would be like if the problem he/she is facing were suddenly gone.
Scaling questions - a tool where clients rate the problem in varying degrees of severity in order to set goals and facilitate change.

SKILL 8.3 Application of Counseling Theories and Techniques to a Specific Situation

Although there are a number of students who need counseling for emotional issues and/or have serious issues in their personal life, these problems usually come to the attention of school personnel when the child runs into trouble academically or displays disruptive classroom behavior. Once a student meets with the counselor, problems of a personal nature may be revealed. Addressing these problems within the context of the goal of success in school is part of the counselor's role.

In the following case study, a student has been referred to the counselor because of poor performance. We will see what happens in the counseling situation to better understand what is going on with the student and how resolution was achieved.

In October Donna, a fifteen year old ninth grader, was referred to the school counselor because she was failing her first year algebra course. The teacher did not feel she was capable of doing the work and was suggesting that she drop the course and go into a general math class instead. This would fulfill her math requirement for high school graduation and she would not be behind one year in math. Donna objected to the move. Her parents wanted her to go to college and general math did not meet the requirements for college entrance. Donna had done well in middle school earning grades of 80's and 85's in eighth grade math. Her test scores on diagnostic math tests in May of the previous year when she was in eighth grade, indicated she performed at a 9.3 grade level.

TEACHER CERTIFICATION STUDY GUIDE

Donna's mother was contacted by telephone and told of the teacher's concern. The mother felt Donna could do the work, that she was lazy and did not apply herself. In discussing with Donna her feelings about why she was failing, the counselor found Donna did not complete her homework assignments because she said when she ran into problems she had no way of solving them. When told she could come in after school for additional help from the teacher Donna said that the days the teacher had designated for extra help were days she had soccer practice.

In discussing a plan for Donna to be successful on the next unit exam in three weeks, it emerged that Donna participated in many non- school activities. She took dance lessons, was out of the house two nights a week for church meetings and to volunteer at the local nursing home reading to elderly patients. She had soccer games on the weekends and her family visited an ailing grandparent on Sundays. Donna had an older sister in her freshman year in college at a school out of town. Her father owned his own business and was active in local politics, and her mother was a teacher.

It was obvious to the counselor that Donna was juggling too many activities and did not have a block of time to devote to her studies. Although she was not failing any of her other courses, her grades were not high enough for entrance into the college that her sister attended and which her parents wanted her to attend. The problem as the counselor saw it was that Donna not only wanted to please her parents by participating in all the out of school activities, but her self esteem and self confidence were derived from these activities. She enjoyed them and did not want to give them up. She continued to think that she could pass the course simply by passing the final exam in June, a school policy.

The counselor decided to use reality therapy with Donna. Donna had a study hall one period a day. She and the counselor decided to use this time for counseling and the teaching of study techniques in the counselor's office. Donna liked this idea as she realized she was not getting any studying done in the study hall because of the disruptive behavior of some of the other students. It was decided Donna and the counselor would talk for twenty minutes and Donna would do her math work for another twenty minutes. Since Donna did not have the time to see the teacher after school, a student from the honor society would come into the guidance office for twenty minutes every other day to help her study her math. Donna was pleased with this arrangement as the immediate problem of math was being addressed.

SCHOOL COUNSELING

In the twenty minutes of counseling time the counselor focused on Donna's lifestyle. Donna had a need to keep busy every minute, the inability to say "no" to many of the projects her parents suggested she do after school, and she had feelings of guilt for her own need to sometimes just do nothing. It was difficult for Donna to accept the fact that she was not able to juggle all these activities, and do well in all of them. She also struggled with the reality that she needed to be able to prioritize and think through what she felt was important in her life, rather than relying on her parents to make these decisions for her. As she began to understand and do better in her algebra class, she continued to feel she could still participate in all her activities.

After Thanksgiving the honor society tutor could no longer help Donna as she needed the time to fill out her own college applications. During the time between Thanksgiving break and Christmas break, Donna's grades in algebra dropped to failing. Donna began to realize even though she could do the math work, as evidenced by her ability to raise her grades when she had the tutor, she could not do it and still maintain her present lifestyle. She needed the discipline to sit down and concentrate. She appealed to the counselor for help in resolving this problem. The counselor began to see a break in Donna's attitude as Donna acknowledged that she needed to change her behavior patterns.

A plan was drawn up for Donna to make time for studying. She decided she would not try out for softball in the spring and would use that time to study and bring her overall grades up. Donna was concerned about telling her parents that she was not going to play softball. A meeting was arranged to present her decision to her parents. At the meeting Donna's parents were surprised and hurt that she had not confided in them. They felt she had been the one who chose to be constantly busy. They did not realize that she felt that her parents demanded the high activity level. The family redefined their goals.

The counselor continued to see Donna throughout the school year. Although Donna and her parents worked at improving her study habits and her priorities, on occasion she slipped, and periodically needed to recommit herself to her original plan. The counselor's support was crucial to Donna's eventual success.

TEACHER CERTIFICATION STUDY GUIDE

OBJECTIVE 0009 Understand a variety of counseling strategies.

SKILL 9.1 Effective Communication Skills

Effective communication is essential to the school counselor's ability to do her or his job successfully. The need to listen and respond well cannot be overestimated. Good communication is not only important in order to meet the needs of the students, but also to enhance the functioning of the guidance department and the school's capacity to respond to student needs.

Equally important is the modeling that effective communication provides to students. Good role models are invaluable to students of all ages. When the school counselor shows students how to pay attention to others, express ideas and opinions, make suggestions, and ask questions clearly and respectfully, he or she is teaching skills that students can use throughout their lifetimes.

The essential elements to effective communication are these:

- Listening attentively without interrupting.

- Responding in ways that the speaker knows that she or he has been heard, including direct appreciation and validation of the speaker's views.

- Articulating ideas, opinions, observations and questions clearly and directly.

- Seeking clarification rather than making assumptions about what the other person is saying.

- Maintaining an attitude of respect at all times, including word usage, voice tone, facial expressions and other non-verbal behavior.

- Working to manage one's emotional reactions so they don't interfere with good communication (e.g., not taking other people's comments personally).

Listening and Responding Skills

Listening is a highly subjective and selective activity. Listening is not just hearing words but grasping the meaning the speaker wishes to impart when those words are uttered. The meaning of the words spoken and interpreted depends upon the subjective world of both the speaker and the listener.

Some barriers to good listening are the following:

1. Hearing what you want to hear, not what is actually said.

2. Not hearing what is said at all due to one's own need to speak. Waiting for the other person to finish so we can speak causes us to think about what we are going to say instead of listening to what is being said.

3. We exhibit biased listening when we form an opinion about the value of what is being said and therefore discount the meaning of the words.

4. Emotions, either negative or positive can cause interference with our listening abilities.

5. The presence of both internal and external distractions.

Elements of Good Listening Skills

Effective listening not only involves tuning into the spoken words of the speaker but perceiving the tone of voice, the nonverbal cues given by the speaker and the emphasis given to the words. A good listener is one who consistently, under many circumstances, accurately understands the speaker's meaning by using their listening skills together with their thinking processes.

Lyman Steil developed the SIER Model which includes four stages of listening. These are *sensing,* the attending to a stimulus; *interpreting,* assigning meaning to incoming information; *evaluating* the message by forming a judgment about what is heard; and finally *responding* to the message.

Good listening skills include the following:

1. Create a positive atmosphere by being alert, attentive, and concentrating on the speaker.

2. Make eye contact and maintaining an expression of genuine interest.

3. Allow the speaker to finish a thought before responding.

4. Avoid critical judgments in your responses.

5. Make an effort to remember what has been said.

6. Avoid changing the subject unless there is a really good reason to do so. When you must change the subject, explain the reason for the change to the speaker.

7. Be as physically relaxed as possible, as such posture communicates that you have time to listen and are interested.

Elements of Good Responding Skills

There are a number of ways one can learn to respond to a speaker to let them know you have heard what he or she is trying to say. If you have listened well and thoughtfully to what the person is saying, your response will be appropriate, you will give good feedback and the speaker will feel good about the fact that you have heard what was said. Good responding skills include:

1. Clarify the meaning of what was said by checking assumptions you have made as the listener to be sure you understand.

2. Continue to maintain eye contact as you give feedback.

3. Keep anger and other emotions out of the interaction. Try to express your feelings in a non-threatening way.

4. Help the other person in problem solving by responding positively and asking good questions.

5. Directly express your appreciation of the speaker's ideas, even if you disagree with them. You can address disagreements more effectively once you have thanked the speaker for sharing his/her ideas.

6. Be physically alert and use appropriate body language.

7. Reflect the person's feelings back to them.

8. Summarize the major ideas and concepts for further clarifications.

9. Use verbal and nonverbal reinforcers (such as head nods) to let the speaker know his/her message has been received.

10. Maintain a comfortable social distance.

11. Give constructive feedback: this is feedback that is descriptive not evaluative, offered not imposed, and focused on behavior rather than personal characteristics. Pay attention to the timing of feedback as well.

These websites offer useful tips on listening and responding skills: www.taft.cc.ca.us/lrc/class/assignments/actlisten.html, crs.uvm.edu/gopher/nerl/personal/comm/e.html, www.nasua.org/informationandreferral/TipSheet1ActiveListening.pdf , and www.psu.edu/dus/cfe/actvlstn.htm.

SKILL 9.2　Resources for Counseling Activities

There are many sources of information that can support counseling activities. Some useful sources are detailed below.

A. Current Professional Journals

The counselor should belong to professional organizations such as the local and state branches of the American Counseling Association and the American School Counselors Association, teacher organizations that relate to their work in developmental areas such as reading and special education, and other broad education organizations such as Phi Delta Kappa. The journals that are published by these organizations have a wealth of information about current trends, theories and practices in the field.

B. Commercial Advertising

Students and parents are bombarded with commercial advertising that often involve education programs. It is important that the counselor is aware of these programs and evaluates them. Many times students look to the counselor to determine the legitimacy of these offers. Advertisements for scholarship searches, tutoring services and computer programs for improvement of grades are some of the ways advertisers entice parents and students to buy their products.

C. Publishing Houses

Once the counselor is registered as a licensed professional, he/she will receive solicitations for new publications, new programs and memberships in related organizations. While there is a tendency to toss all this information into the trash, some of it is valuable and should at least be perused. A system can be devised among counseling staff for each counselor to be responsible for specific areas and to share this pertinent material at staff meetings.

D. College and Military Base Visits

In order to keep up with new programs colleges are offering to students and to become familiar with the admissions staff at the different institutions, it is important for the counselor to visit these schools, and, at least once a year, take an out of area visit to schools in which some of their students have taken an interest. Quite often students are unable to visit a school before applying and the counselor visitation can help a particular student by providing information about the characteristics of that school. The armed forces offer trips to military installations to familiarize the counselor with the educational programs of the particular branch of the service represented. These are usually free or low cost. The school district may be persuaded to provide funds from the guidance budget for some of these visitations.

E. College Night

A joint college night sponsored by all the schools in the county can be both a service to the students and a possible fund raiser. If the colleges are charged a small fee for presenting and if a dinner is provided, the counselors can raise money for scholarships for needy and deserving students. It is also good public relations for the department when they can present a scholarship to a student at the awards night program.

F. Visits to Other School Programs

Counselors can learn from innovative programs instituted by other schools by visiting these programs and evaluating their good and bad aspects. After a program has been in practice for a period of time, the originators of the program are aware of improvements that should be made. If your school is interested in starting the program, it can be beneficial to learn from the mistakes of others and to be able to offer an improved version of the program.

G. Workshops and Conventions

Workshops and conventions are a valuable resource for new ideas and innovative practices. They are also a vehicle for learning new state and federal rules and regulations. When a counselor belongs to professional organizations, information about coming events is mailed to the counselor well in advance of the event. The counselor can then choose the event they wish to attend depending on interest and expertise. In addition, counselors who have expertise in a particular area can present at these programs. This gives the counselor the chance to share their ideas with others and also lends a degree of prestige to the school in which they are employed. Local opportunities should not be excluded; nearby colleges or agencies may offer relevant continuing education programs as well as the chance to network with potential referrals.

SKILL 9.3   Communicating Information to Students

The major task of the counselor in the school is communication: with the student, the parent/guardian, teachers, school administrators and support staff members, other professionals, people in the community and sometimes even members of the media. The primary client, however, is the student.

The ability to create rapport and meaningful relationships with students and others is the sign of an effective counselor. When the counselor has the trust of the student, the student is much more likely to listen to and act on the counselor's suggestions. Keeping information confidential, within the confines of the need for parental notification and other school policies, is essential to building trust.

If the counselor does not keep information confidential, trust is destroyed, and it is harder to help the student grow and mature. Trust is built up gradually. In order to facilitate trust, information given to the student must always be true, accurate and timely. The counselor must be a visible presence in the school, and be available to students. There are many ways to make contact with students, both formally and informally. When such an atmosphere of accessibility is created, students will be much more inclined to contact the counselor in time of need and crisis.

A. Newsletters

Monthly newsletters to a student's home inform the student and the parent/guardian about what is happening in the world of guidance. Newsletters should contain deadline dates for national exams, dates of specific college visitations, notice of aptitude and school generated exams, scholarship deadlines, workshops about financial, and other items of interest that are occurring in the Guidance Department and the community at large. It may feature some of the guidance clerical staff and their duties, procedures for making appointments with the staff and any other information that would facilitate connection and communication. If the principal or other school administrator sends out a monthly bulletin, a section of that newsletter could be set aside for guidance news.

B. Homeroom and Classroom Visitations

Visiting homerooms is an efficient way for counselors to get to know students, . Students are also able to ask questions or be reminded of issues they may wish to discuss with the counselor. It is helpful for students to see counselors in various settings throughout the school so they don't associate the counselor only with problems or trouble.

Visiting the classroom is also a means of disseminating information directly to students. For example, when it comes time to schedule the high school student for the following year, the homeroom visiting the homeroom (or other classes such as social sciences) creates an opportunity to share the course schedule and other information efficiently.

C. Individual Interviews

Much of the real work of counseling occurs in the individual interviews the counselor holds with the student. These interviews should occur on a regular basis although this may be challenging when the counselor's caseload is high. At the high school level, freshmen and seniors should be scheduled as soon as possible within the first month of school. For freshmen, the interview is a chance to get acquainted and find out if there are any adjustment problems; for seniors, the discussion serves to inform them about post-secondary training and college application deadlines, tests needed for entrance to college, and other plans for post high school activities. The initial interviews with freshmen can also help create the basis of trust needed to help students with future problems.

D. Dissemination of Forms

Each school has systematic ways to distribute necessary information to students. This might include applications for national exams, local and state scholarships, as well as other guidance-related material. Some schools utilize the homeroom setting; others send home this information to individual students or give it out in individual interviews. Quite often the counselor has access to a large group of students during a study hall period or in the cafeteria. A study hall situation may offer an ideal chance for answering questions about testing and other issues students wish to discuss.

E. Intercom Announcements

Announcements over the school intercom system are an excellent vehicle to remind students of guidance and other activities that are occurring on a specific day. It is also a means of informing students of upcoming activities and deadline dates.

F. Informal Chance Meetings

It is important that the counselor get out of the office some time during the school day to meet students in areas they frequent during their time at school. The cafeteria, the hallways, and the student lounge are all places the counselor can meet students, ask how they are doing, remind them of specific issues and make appointments for meetings.

SKILL 9.4 Conducting an Orientation Program to the School and Guidance Program

A major change in the life of a child is the transition from home to school. For the student entering school for the first time, as well as the transitions from elementary to middle school, and middle school to high school, a smooth and anxiety-reducing procedure can be extremely useful. While the attitude of the parent/guardian is important, the school people the child has first contact with sets the tone for the school experience. Therefore, it is important that the organizers of the first encounter recognize the needs of the child and address these fears and needs through a student orientation.

Careful planning is essential. A written procedure to eliminate the possibility of omitting details important to the success of the orientation helps. Details include:

1. Parents receive advance notification of the time, date, and place of the orientation. The notice should include a student handbook with the school regulations clearly spelled out as well as penalties for infractions of the school rules.

2. The meeting is set for the early evening and lasts no more than an hour and one half.

3. The agenda for the meeting is carefully delineated ahead of time and at the meeting.

4. The principal and other school administrators are introduced, and their role in the school community explained.

5. The Guidance Department introduces its staff members, and explains the functions and programs of the department, including the procedures for seeing a counselor.

6. There should be a question and answer period that is restricted in duration.

7. At the middle and high school levels, discuss scheduling and give all students copies of their schedules. Additional copies should be available on the first day for the students who have not brought their copy to school.

8. A tour of the facilities can be conducted by upper class students to help the new students familiarize themselves with the building and the rooms in which their classes will be held.

9. If possible, refreshments should be served, with parents, students, and staff mingling in an informal atmosphere.

TEACHER CERTIFICATION STUDY GUIDE

OBJECTIVE 0010   Understand group dynamics and principles of group counseling.

SKILL 10.1   Merits and Limitations of Group Counseling

Both group and individual counseling require the counselor have knowledge of the theoretical basis of counseling. All major counseling theories can be applied to both situations. During group counseling, the theories take on a more social nature. The theoretical method chosen depends upon the orientation of the counselor, the needs of the client(s), and the goals of the counseling process.

Merits of Group Counseling

In a group situation, members have the ability, in a safe and non-threatening atmosphere, to test their attitudes and beliefs against those of the other members of the group. They can receive feedback and discover how they are viewed by others. The group setting can also be a support system for its members, and may be particularly important when members have no other means of emotional support. In this way they can achieve and experiment with some of the goals of becoming emotionally involved without the threat of rejection.

A counseling group is made up of various members of society and thus can be a representation of the client's outer world – the world outside the counseling room. Members can experiment with their styles of interaction with other people in a contained, managed environment. They can then transfer these techniques and behaviors into real life situations. Members of the group can, as they process the observations of the group and their own reactions to others, get a better idea of who they want to become, as well as a better understanding of their own behavior.

For the counselor, the advantages of groups include the ability to reach more clients, to become familiar with differing populations of the school community, and to become more aware of current trends in youth culture.

Limitations of Group Counseling

There may be a tendency to view group counseling as a quick, easy solution when in fact the counselor may find that the work load preparation has increased in proportion to the number of members in the group. Often, individual members need different theoretical approaches as well as extended follow-up.

There is tremendous pressure to accept the group values and substitute them for the previous unworkable value system instead of forming new sets of approaches to the old problem.

Some people function poorly in the group situation. For one reason or another they cannot accept the group's perceptions and fall further into a psychological "funk". Some may find the group setting threatening in spite of the counselor's efforts to create a safe environment.

The personality or acute life circumstances of some individuals may prevent them from making changes in their lives. They may use the group to justify their present status and therefore do not gain from the group's insights.

An excellent resource on all aspects of group counseling is *The Theory and Practice of Group Psychotherapy* by Yalom and Leszcz (2005).

For more information about group counseling, see www.agpa.org/guidelines/factorsandmechanisms.html.

SKILL 10.2 Group Dynamics

Understanding group dynamics is based on knowledge about the psychological and social forces inherent within groups. These forces operate in all human interactions. Over the last fifty years, the concept of group dynamics has become more developed and there exist a number of definitions of group dynamics.

One definition states that group dynamics is a political ideology that is built upon the concept of the organization and management of the group. It emphasizes democratic leadership, equality of membership in decision making and the benefits of group interaction to both society in general and the individual members specifically. Critics of this definition say the emphasis on the group is a method of operating rather than a way of understanding the goals and purpose of the group.

A second definition of group dynamics is derived from the techniques used in group process. Some of these techniques include role-playing, observation and feedback from group members, the decision making process and the concept of "buzz sessions". This type of group process was developed at the National Training Laboratory (www.ntl.org), among other places.

The third definition of group dynamics encompasses the entire field of research and application concerning the nature of groups, the history of their development and their interrelations with individuals, other groups and established institutions. This is the most accepted definition of group dynamics at this time, with a focus on human behavior and relationships.

Some distinctive aspects of the study of group dynamics include:

1. **The emphasis on both theoretical significance and empirical research.** Originally functions of group life were debated in an intellectual setting without the benefit of empirical data. These ideas were based upon personal experience projected into general theories. By the 1920's, scholars in psychology and sociology began thinking in empirical terms. They started to seek facts based on objective data rather than subjective impressions. They sought data that could be reproduced by other researchers. Consequently, group dynamics research evolved as a phenomenon that could be observed, quantified, measured and experimented. However, such research is highly complex since it involves a number of individuals and many variables, so it is difficult to actually prove many concepts scientifically. Therefore group dynamics research still depends heavily on theory.

2. **Interest in the interdependence of phenomena.** This refers to the concept that observations of the group depend upon what new phenomena would be created from other conditions yet to be observed. While looking for general principles about what conditions produce what effects, much is not known about the interdependence of different conditions upon the dynamics of the group. Some of these complicated questions include the results of change, resistance to change, social pressures, influence, coercion, power and instability.

3. **Interdisciplinary relevance.** Sociologists, psychologists, cultural anthropologists, political scientists and economists all have an interest in the dynamics of group interaction, as their studies include the behavior of groups. Therefore, general knowledge about the interaction and dynamics of groups touches upon many social science disciplines.

4. **Potential application of findings to social practice.** The goal of those studying group dynamics is to help improve the functioning of groups for both societal and individual benefit. Many diverse professions such as labor-management mediation, marriage counseling, and pastoral counseling have much to gain from the scientific study of groups. Supervisors in any profession who have responsibility for other individuals also need this knowledge base. Many training centers have emerged in response to these professionals' need for accurate and effective ways of dealing with groups.

School counselors have many opportunities to utilize knowledge of group dynamics. In the classroom setting, in group counseling, and in understanding the dynamics of peer groups, counselors can draw on understanding how groups affect individual students' behavior. Always being mindful of the power of groups to affect individuals can be an asset in many school counselor functions.

OBJECTIVE 0011 Understand principles for developing and implementing classroom guidance curricula.

SKILL 11.1 Developing Special Programs to Meet Identified Needs

Although many of the school counselor's tasks are designated by the overall plan of the guidance program, there is occasionally the need to develop special programs to cope with an emerging problem or respond to a particular group of students. Such a need may be identified by a formal needs assessment or, more commonly, by a classroom management problem, teacher observations or direct knowledge of the counselor. A specific program to address the need can be a creative solution and serve to prevent an escalation of the problem.

Two examples of special programs are the Lunch Bunch and an anger management mini-group. The Lunch Bunch is an opportunity for new students to meet with other students new to the district and the counselor in a small group at lunch time. Meeting in a somewhat informal setting while eating lunch can be useful and non-threatening for new students. It addresses the discomfort some students feel at lunch time when long-time friends sit together. It helps build peer relationships as well as a connection with the school counselor. It can, after a few meetings, include "old" students to help the students build bridges into the larger school community. The Lunch Bunch should only meet short-term (4-6 times) once a week at the same time, in order to facilitate this process of integration.

A psycho-educational group focused on anger management can be an opportunity for violence and bullying prevention as well as an intervention strategy. In this setting (which is more formal than the Lunch Bunch, for example) the school counselor meets with a small group (6-8) of students who need help with anger management skills. They can be self-selected or identified by the counselor, teachers and other staff. In this group, skills are taught and information shared. Behavior modification approaches may also be employed. Further, students can discuss their concerns about and struggles with anger and other emotions.

Ideally, the school counselor has students complete evaluation forms following their involvement in such special programs, in order to assess their effectiveness. This information could be used in deciding to offer the program again, modifying the program or developing new programs. Other staff members and teachers who are involved in the program or are able to observe the effects of the program may also be solicited for their feedback.

TEACHER CERTIFICATION STUDY GUIDE

SKILL 11.2 Basic Prevention Concepts and Other Curricular Strategies

In addition to providing counseling after a problem has been identified, it is the task of the school counselor to contribute to the school's effort to prevent difficulties before they arise. Central to the notion of prevention is the importance of creating a positive school environment (see Skill 4.1). Further, as noted previously, attending to issues of bullying, prejudice, aggression and violence in the school setting are key to preventing problems. Teaching communication, self-awareness and conflict resolution skills to students are also effective prevention approaches.

Other key prevention concepts include the following ideas:

Maintain an open door policy. Students need to know that the school counselor is there to help. An attitude of openness and positive communication can encourage students to seek assistance when something concerns them before it escalates into a larger problem.

Create a student assistance team (SAP). By designating and training a group of teachers and staff (counselors, psychologist, nurse, social worker, etc.) as people students can go to when they are experiencing difficulties, the school offers students the opportunity to get the help they need to be successful in school. SAPs provide early intervention and referral, and have the advantage of being interdisciplinary and collaborative.

Implement programs that involve students in the school community in innovative ways. By engaging students in programs beyond the scope of the classroom and traditional guidance functions, they become invested in the larger school community. This enhances their self-esteem and helps forge new bonds among students. At times, peers are able to help students when adults are less able to do so. Attention needs to be given to recruitment of students for such programs, and adequate orientation, training and supervision must be provided.

Such programs might include the following:

1. **Cross-age teaching:** Have high school students help with programs for elementary and middle school students. These could involve tutoring, conflict resolution, peer mediation, or orientation for students moving from one school building to the next.

2. **New student welcoming committee:** Establish a group of students who are willing to mentor students new to the district. They can sit with their mentees at lunch and share information about the school. New friendships may develop, and both mentors and mentees have the chance to meet people who are perhaps different from them.

SCHOOL COUNSELING

3. **Service clubs:** Sponsor or help start a service club oriented to helping students implement projects that improve the school and community environment. Some examples are a recycling project within the school, a holiday gift program for needy families, and a volunteer program to help the elderly in the community or to bring seasonal artwork to nursing home patients.

4. **Student involvement in the guidance program:** Inviting students to help out with guidance activities such as Career Day or Financial Aid Night or with office tasks can be worthwhile to students who are interested.

TEACHER CERTIFICATION STUDY GUIDE

CONSULTATION AND COLLABORATION:
OBJECTIVES 0012-0015

OBJECTIVE 0012 Understand theories, models, and processes of consultation and strategies for collaborating with teachers and other school personnel.

SKILL 12.1 Components of a Consultation Prototype

The purpose of all consultation procedures is to problem-solve. The principals in the consultation process are the consultant, usually the counselor in a school setting, but could also be a person knowledgeable in the problem at hand, and the consultee, often a teacher or other school personnel. The consultee is not usually the student whose problem is the topic of discussion. Although the student has a vital part in the process, the purpose of the consultation is to aid the consultee in solving a problem that usually concerns a student or a group of students. In the school setting, consultees can be one or more school personnel, and consultants can be more than one person with knowledge of the student and/or expertise in the solving of this particular problem.

Most often the consultation process is used to solve an academic problem of a student. However, school problems increasingly involve difficulties of a societal nature that affect the school environment and school population as a whole. Often problems from outside the school setting spill over into the school, disrupting the learning atmosphere. School policy issues are often solved by employing the consultation model. Some examples of these issues are dress codes, drug policies, and issues of sudden death in the school community. Different approaches are used depending upon the particular goal of the consultant and consultee.

The consultant can take the role of an **advocate** in directly presenting evidence and attempting to persuade the consultee to take some stand or action. The advocacy can be in support of a student, a group of students or an idea to be implemented.

The consultant can also act in the capacity of an **expert** in a particular field. This role is employed when there is a need to inform or educate the consultee in a specialized area. For the school counselor this may take the form of interpretation of test data, psychological and environmental background information or placement data.

Another role of the consultant would entail specific **training and education** in an area such as identifying "children at risk." The goal here is to develop school-wide plans and procedures to solve the problem of, for example, the rate of drop outs.

TEACHER CERTIFICATION STUDY GUIDE

The counselor/consultant's role most often used in the school setting is that of **consultant/collaborator** where the consultee and the consultant's roles are equal in attempting to solve the problem. It is a three pronged relationship; the counselor/consultant, the teacher/consultee and the client system (which can include the student and the student's parents). In the role as a collaborator the counselor takes part of the responsibility for implementing the plan to solve the problem. This may take on the role of directly working with the student to reinforce behavior change.

The task of **fact finding** (gathering relevant information, studying it and disseminating it to the consultee) falls upon the shoulders of the consultant. Finally the role the consultant can take is that of the **process specialist**, in which the counselor outlines the steps needed to reach mutual goals.

There is a common procedure for all consultation processes, although the settings in which the consultation takes place may differ. Some of these places are:

1. A clinical setting which can be a mental health facility.
2. A school setting with the parent, teacher or administrator present.
3. A training setting for education purposes.
4. A school or business with the staff of an organization.

Prior to the first session, the consultant should gather certain data. These include background information as to the purpose of the consultation process, some of the political considerations of the process (when applicable), and other facts that may help the consultant in understand the dynamics of the situation.

The goals of the consultation should be formulated so that all concerned parties know where the process is headed. The function, role, techniques and procedures used by the consultant in the consultation process should be formulated after the above issues are determined.

The experience of the consultee in the consultation process should be taken into consideration so that if additional education and skill training are required the consultant is prepared to furnish that training.

Some of the common procedures for all consultation processes are as follows:

A. Entry - Relationship Building

In using the school setting as the basis for consultation we most often are involved in attempting to change student behavior. It is essential to obtain the trust and confidence of the student and to motivate the student to change. The student, although not always directly involved in the strategies to be employed in attempting to change behavior, must be informed and give useful information.

SCHOOL COUNSELING

Further, the student needs to cooperate in the plans for implementing the behavior change. This is absolutely essential for the process to be successful. When this is done the consultant can then proceed in implementing the process of consultation by contacting other parties involved, such as the child's parents, teachers, experts in areas of special needs and any other support personnel deemed important in solving the problem. As far as possible, the student should be included in defining the problem with the consultee, especially at the secondary level, and should also be included in meetings during which the strategies to be used are developed.

B. Diagnosis and Definition of Problem

It should be clear to all participants what has been diagnosed as the problem. Quite often the consultee and the student see the problem in different lights and therefore a plan to solve the problem cannot work if the student and consultee are at odds. In a situation where a student needs to modify behavior, the model of **behavior consultation,** based on the theory of social learning, is employed. Specific changes in behavior are sought. Information regarding the problem is obtained; the problem is defined in detail; goals are set; plan strategies are developed; assessment criteria are agreed upon; and avenues of intervention are explored. Solving the problem depends upon the consultee "making it happen"; therefore, it is critical that the consultee has ownership of the plan.

Other models of consultation are **organization consultation** where the problem is in the organizational framework. This is most often used when an expert in that particular area is required. The **doctor/patient** model is when an organization knows there is a problem but does not know the nature of the problem. When the interactions of the members of an organization are examined, **process consultation** is employed. When the mental health of a community can be improved by consulting with other human services professionals in the delivery of their services, **mental health consultation** is employed.

C. Devising and Implementing a Plan

In devising a plan, the counselor/consultant, together with the student and the consultee (teacher), identify a behavior that is of most concern to all. A plan of action is devised as to how to expedite change with equal input from all participants involved. Techniques of encouragement, logical consequences, praise and reward are used to reach goals set down by all parties. The consultant needs to monitor the process and identify problems with the implementation so the plan can be changed if necessary.

D. Evaluation and Summarization

Although the initial meeting is usually not the only meeting, a summary of what has transpired during the meeting should be made before terminating the session. Each participant should fully understand their role in implementing behavior change and should be held responsible for his/her part in the process. Once the behavior change has been accomplished, an evaluation of the process should be made by the consultant.

SKILL 12.2   Strategies for Effective Consultation

Assist Participants in Problem Solving

The counselor/consultant should have a plan of action to assist the participants in doing their parts in effecting change. This can take the role of teaching specific skills, as in the case of a teacher with no prior experience in attempting behavior change, or in helping the teacher devise strategies and sequential plans to deal with the defined behavior problem. The consultant should be able to help the consultee describe in detail the specific types of behavior that are problematic. If necessary, the consultant should make arrangements for any clerical help needed in order to relieve the teacher/consultee of this task.

Help should also be provided to the student and his/her parents in order for the consultation to affect the desired change in behavior. This should take the form of frequent contact to evaluate the progress of the process and to ascertain if more aid is needed or additional concerns on the part of the student and parent have arisen.

Communicate the Needs of the Student

It is important for the consultant not to assume what the needs of the student are without first clarifying those needs directly with the student. In the case of an adolescent, if this is not done first, trust will not be attained and the whole process is likely to fail. Permission to share these needs should be obtained from the student in order to reinforce the trust relationship.

Once this is done, a meeting should be held with the consultee to communicate these needs. If the student can be present, misunderstandings are less likely to occur. Such a meeting can also be a method to open lines of further dialogue between the student and the consultee. In this scenario the consultant acts in part as the advocate of the student/client using expertise acquired from experience. It is important the consultant balance the needs of the student/client with those of the consultee/teacher in order to achieve maximum results.

Involve Parent/Guardian(s) in Consultation

Parent/guardian(s) are a vital part of the consultation process. Consultation works best when the parent/guardian(s) are involved in the consultation process from the beginning. Even in the case of non-cooperative parents the consultant must inform them every step of the way. Often the situation is complicated by divorced and separated families, issues of custody, and the alienation of the student from his family. The consultant, while respecting the parent/guardian(s)'s rights, must always keep in mind the primary goal of solving the student's problem.

See Skill 13.2 for more information about involving parent/guardian(s) in the consultation process.

Assist in the Use of Data and Resources

The consultant needs to have as much information about the situation and the student as possible. Do not rush into the consultation process without doing an adequate job of gathering data. Some of the things the consultant can do are:

1. Examine the permanent record for standardized test scores, patterns of grade fluctuation, weak and strong areas, and attendance record.

2. Talk with the present teacher(s) to ascertain if they are all having the same problem, and if not, gather insights from the teacher who is not having a problem.

3. Observe the student in the classroom, if possible.

4. Administer additional tests if necessary.

5. Gather medical, physical and discipline history.

Once you have some kind of analysis of the possible problem, compile a list of resources that might be available, both in and outside the school community, to be used as support mechanisms. This list may include:

- short or long term personal counseling, both for the student and the family
- alcohol and other drug counseling
- academic tutoring
- referral to the school psychologist for special education testing
- school social worker intervention for family visits and ongoing support

This list should be available when the consultation process begins, so if needed, action can be taken at that time.

Identify Procedures for Transition and Follow-Up

When it has been determined that the consultation process has been successful in solving the problem, a formal evaluation of the process is in order. This can be accomplished by a number of methods. Individual interviews with all parties involved in the process can be conducted or a survey instrument used to determine if the consultee and the student/client have been satisfied with the process. Input concerning the areas they feel need to be continued or modified, the process for the continuation of the plan, and comments relating to the entire procedure should also be solicited.

The consultant becomes increasingly less active in the consultation process as part of the transition phase, agreeing to decrease and eliminate the need for intervention in a gradual way. As a final step, after the consultant has not been involved for a period of time, a follow-up interview should be conducted as to the effectiveness of the process. If there is a regression on the part of the student/client, it may be appropriate to reinstitute the consultation process or make further referrals.

OBJECTIVE 0013 *Understand strategies for consulting and collaborating with families and community agencies to provide an effective support system for students.*

SKILL 13.1 **Knowledge of Family Dynamics**

Families of students may consist of a variety of people besides a mother, father and siblings. This is especially true of families who have experienced the disruption of divorce, death, homelessness, natural disasters, mental health and addiction problems and other issues. Being alert to the various configurations of "family" is crucial to effectively serving students and families.

Awareness of the issues that particular families face as outlined in Skill 2.3 (Special Populations) is also essential. The stresses on many families impair their abilities to support students adequately, and sensitivity on the part of school counselors to these issues can be useful. This awareness can help by avoiding stigma and further stress as well as serving to ameliorate the existing stress by providing support and resources.

While counselors often find they need to serve as an advocate for students with colleagues, parents, and care providers, school counselors also may need to advocate for parents and guardians at times. Thinking of oneself as an advocate for families as well as for individual students can be beneficial. This stance is useful both in fostering positive relationships with parents and guardians, but also in producing positive results for the student.

Contributions from the Field of Family Therapy

Family therapy is a branch of counseling that addresses the well-being of families. It developed in the 1950's as a way to help families make changes in their functioning. Although it is beyond the scope of the job of school counselors to work with families in a therapeutic context, the field of family therapy has some useful insights for school counselors. This information can help counselors better understand and interact with family members in their efforts to help students succeed in school and life.

Family therapists draw on various theories and counseling approaches, including group dynamics, systems theory, psychodynamic theory and therapy, Gestalt, cognitive-behavioral therapy, object relations, narrative therapy and solution-focused therapy. They may have a background in child development, social work or psychology. What they agree on is that the family is the primary group within which each person learns how to behave with others.

Specifically, family therapy suggests that an individual's behavior derives from and is maintained not only by early family and caregiver experiences but by current experiences with whomever he or she perceives as family. Other people's behavior helps keep an individual acting in certain ways. Further, these interactions are often repetitive and circular, reinforcing each other. Therefore, in some cases, interventions need to include family members so that an individual is able to make behavioral changes.

Another contribution from family therapy is the understanding that there are overt and covert roles and rules that guide behavior in families. Family members may or may not be consciously aware of these parameters, but their behavior is still affected by them. In rigid families, any deviation from these rules and roles can cause distress in other family members and in the system as a whole. This reactivity can keep family members, especially children, from changing their behavior, even in other settings.

How families manage conflict is often a characteristic that defines a particular family. Some families avoid conflict at all costs; others seem to thrive on patterns of conflict. Often, "problem" children or adolescents (known as "the identified patient" in family therapy jargon) serve to keep the parents from addressing underlying issues. This conflict focuses family concern away from a more painful problem, almost always one that is grounded in the adult relationship(s).

More information about family therapy can be located at these websites: www.familytherapyresources.net/, www.mayoclinic.com, and en.wikipedia.org/wiki/Family_therapy,

SKILL 13.2   Parents and Guardians as Partners

Understanding the Needs of Parent/Guardian(s)

Parents and legal guardians are the people with whom school counselors are most likely to interact. In fact, without the express consent of parents and guardians, counselors are not permitted to discuss the student with any other family members.

Having an understanding of what parents and guardians need can be helpful in developing and maintaining positive relationships with parents and guardians. The three basic things that parents need from school counselors are respect, validation and support, and information.

Respect

As noted previously (see Skill 2.4), respect is a key element in effective communication. Parents and guardians may or may not be respectful of school personnel. The parents' history with members of the school community, their own experiences as a student, the current stresses in their lives and their general approach to life may influence how they respond to school counselors. Nonetheless, it is essential that counselors act respectfully in all of their interactions with parents and guardians.

Respect is conveyed through word choice, voice tone, and content. Positive, inclusive statements express respect. Questions that invite collaboration also suggest respect. A lack of reactivity helps maintain respectful interactions. Counselors need to remember that some people respond to any contact by someone from their child's school with fear and/or anger. Being non-reactive to the parent's response will aid the counselor in communicating respect and concern, and helps avoid unnecessary conflict.

Validation and Support

Parents and guardians need validation and support from school counselors, especially when addressing difficult issues. Direct comments such as "I know you want the best for your child" and "I'm sure you are doing your best to help your child" can be useful. It also may be helpful to introduce a sensitive concern with "You probably know this, but I wanted to tell you...." This takes into account that the parent may be aware of what the counselor is going to disclose and communicates that the counselor believes that the parent is tuned into his or her child. While this may not always be the case, it is better to err in this direction.

In spite of any failings, parents and guardians are doing their best. From the counselor's perspective, parents may not be meeting the student's needs. They may even be abusive and neglectful. When necessary, the school counselor may have to directly confront a parent or guardian, or file an abuse report. However, most of the time, parents and guardians are doing the best they can. Support and validation may also aid them in positively changing their behavior.

Information

The third thing parents and guardians need is clear information. The counselor needs to be direct in communicating his or her concerns about the student. As noted, the parent may or may not be aware of what has come to the counselor's attention. Parent/guardians have the right and need to be informed. They also need to hear what the counselor and other school personnel are proposing as an action plan. This information needs to be conveyed in a non-judgmental way, without direct or implied criticism of the parent, even when the counselor is asking the parent to do something differently.

Consultation as the Model for Interacting with Parents and Guardian

A good way to approach working with parents and guardians of students is to think about it as consultation. Interactions with parents and guardians are a two-way street: the counselor has information and concerns to share with the parent or guardian, who also has information and concerns to share with the counselor. A collaborative mindset will aid in eliciting cooperation and engagement with parents, and ultimately leads to the best results for the student.

Parent/guardian(s) are a valuable source of information about the student. Issues of family background and medical history information can only be obtained from parents or those adults who have been privy to family interaction. Such data can be very helpful in generating solutions to the problems the student is encountering in the school setting.

Non-cooperative parents may have an "attitude" about how the school has "not done right by" their child. It is in the best interest of all to permit them to vent their feelings. This may be one of the few times school personnel have listened to them. Emphasize that the school is not giving up on the child, and if in the past strategies for improvement have not worked, new strategies will be developed.

When consulting with parent/guardians, focus on the issue at hand as soon as possible after allowing them to vent. Explain the concerns and the tentative plan to the parents. Enlist the equal cooperation of parents by asking how they feel about the suggested course of action. Accept ideas for modification when appropriate, and help them see that they are a vital part of making the plan work.

Good counselors maintain an openness to possible solutions, modifying action plans as new information is gathered from parents. This openness includes being alert to their own assumptions about what is best for the student and what remedies or support is needed. Such an approach will also communicate to parents their significance and value, further aiding true collaboration.

Be careful not to overwhelm parents and guardians by giving them too many tasks, keeping in mind they may have too much stress in their daily lives already. Encourage them to feel that you, collectively, are developing a workable plan that may need modifying as it progresses. It is important to set up checkpoints to contact them about the progress of the course of action. If additional contact is not made, the parents will be negative about the entire process and further intervention on the part of the school will be extremely difficult.

On a more general level, another avenue to engage parent/guardians as collaborators is to form a parent advisory committee. This group can serve as a resource to the guidance department and help create open channels of communication between school counselors and parent/guardian(s).

SKILL 13.3 Referrals to and Use of External Resources

Referrals to Outside Agencies and Practitioners

Appropriate referrals for students to professional individuals and agencies are procedural functions of both the school district and the specific school in which the counselor works. There is usually a set policy to which a referring counselor must conform. When the decision is made to refer a student for further help

A form should be used to inform the person to whom the student is referred the nature of the problem, along with background information and standardized test scores, what has been tried already, with whom, and what the results are of different strategies employed. Follow-up and further meetings should be held to determine the outcome of the referral. The person to whom the student is referred should also issue a report on the results.

The first step in getting outside help for the student is to get the informed consent of the student and his/her parent/guardian to make the referral. In the case of abuse by a family or household member, the counselor is mandated to report the incident to the proper authorities as well. If a parent or guardian is the abuser it is not prudent to include that person in the referral process. The mandated state organization will approach the parent or guardian.

In the case of alcohol or other drug or emotional problems, the parent/guardian should be included from the start. The question of expense or insurance coverage is a significant factor to be considered. In any case of referral, written documentation should be kept. Personal contact with the agency receiving the referral should be made by the counselor. Regular contact with this individual and the parents should be made until the problem is resolved or the student is no longer enrolled in the school.

It is often helpful to have a form on which to track referrals to outside agencies and individuals. This creates a useful record for accountability purposes and makes follow-up easier.

Support and Resources for Families

The school counselor is often in the position of helping families access resources for purposes other than referrals for evaluative or mental health services. Sometimes the counselor will provide the student with information about resources; other times the counselor will offer referrals to the parents and guardians. Regardless, this requires knowledge of community and internet resources on many different topics including but not limited to financial aid, mental health and social service agencies, vocational training programs, food banks, prevention, support groups, colleges and universities, advocacy networks, government-sponsored aid programs, and enrichment activities.

Networking with community agencies, private practitioners, other school districts, professional associations and local and state education agencies can be useful in gathering resource information. The counselor should maintain a database as well as a file of brochures, business cards and information packets to draw on as needed. It is also helpful to keep a list of contact people at various agencies and programs in order to facilitate referrals and expedite access for families.

TEACHER CERTIFICATION STUDY GUIDE

OBJECTIVE 0014 *Understand crisis intervention strategies for students, families, school, and communities facing emergency situations.*

Skill 14.1 Core Crisis Intervention Concepts

Crisis and emergency situations are events beyond the realm of every day life. They always involve some degree of surprise, shock, loss and emotion. Crises include death, natural disasters such as earthquakes and hurricanes, vehicular and other accidents, school shootings, and other forms of extreme violence. The unpredictability of crises, the experience of loss that invariably accompanies such situations and the strong feelings that are evoked all make crisis and emergency events particularly potent and challenging for everyone involved.

The value of being prepared

Pre-planning and training in basic crisis management skills can be extremely helpful in responding effectively. Although the events themselves may be unpredictable, there is a body of information about how people react to crisis and what responders can do to ameliorate and manage the aftermath of crisis. This is important in school settings, where there are a large number of people congregated in one place and contagion is a concern. Anxiety and misinformation can spread like wildfire, exacerbating the short and long term effects of traumatic events.

Designating and training a crisis response team can be quite beneficial. Comprehensive crisis management training as well as ongoing refresher courses are necessary for a team to function well. In most cases, the school counselor is integrally involved in the work of crisis team. He or she may be a leader or not, depending on the structure of the team, the preferences of the administration, and the background of the counselor.

In addition to a crisis team, school districts need to have clearly defined crisis response plans. They should include as much detail as possible, with specific recommendations for different situations as needed, although a general plan is applicable in many circumstances. The plan should incorporate the following:

- delineate the school's goals in crisis situations (such as maintaining as normal a school day as possible, or providing timely information),
- identify key players on the crisis response team,
- specify how communication will be handled,
- describe what interventions will be used with students,
- note how interactions and referrals to outside agencies will be managed, and
- detail what follow-up is needed.

Further, it helps to have handouts about traumatic stress reactions, sample letters to parents and guardians, press releases (when necessary) and other useful documents ready prior to any event.

The need for information

Everyone who experiences a traumatic event needs to be aware of the normal reactions and common feelings of survivors, as well as receive accurate information about the event itself (when this is not known) and what the school is doing in response. This means that the district needs to make clear decisions about the actions the school is taking, including what parents and guardians need to know and do, and communicate these plans succinctly and in a timely manner to all in the school community. Information also needs to flow to the larger community. Specific, to-the-point information is valuable; avoid all rumors.

Intervention for students

Most commonly, school counselors and other school personnel will be available for crisis counseling and support in a designated room for a day or two after a traumatic event. Some districts will invite local experts in traumatic stress response or grief counseling to come to the school to aid school personnel. Interventions include listening, normalizing the reactions of students, offering to call parents and guardians, and making arrangements for the student to go home early when needed. Referrals to outside professionals may also be made.

Self-care during and after the event

Part of a school crisis plan should spell out how responders and other school personnel will receive and give support during the implementation of the crisis management plan. Further, school counselors and other personnel need to get rest and support after doing crisis response work. This work is very demanding and the effects on responders may not be immediately apparent. Secondary post-traumatic stress is a concern, particularly when the crisis response team has multiple or ongoing situations to manage. Adequate administrative and personal support, time off, and sufficient training and de-briefing are essential.

The following websites have information about school crisis management, traumatic stress reactions, and related topics:

www.nctsnet.org/nccts/nav.do?pid=ctr_aud_schlmeans that part of the crisis response
 www.cdc.gov/niosh/unp-trinstrs.html
 www.aaets.org/trresp.htm
www.apa.org/practice/traumaticstress.html
www.ed.gov/admins/lead/safety/training/responding/crisis_pg11.html?exp=2.

OBJECTIVE 0015 Understand the role of the school counselor as advocate.

Skill 15.1 The school counselor as advocate

An advocate is someone who speaks up for another (usually someone lacking power in a situation) with the goal of making sure that person is heard. Schools are complex systems comprised of many individuals and groups competing for resources and attention. At times, students and/or parents and guardians may not feel their concerns are being acknowledged or addressed. Counselors may also observe ongoing issues with groups of students, or recognize segments of the student body who are not receiving adequate support or services. In these circumstances, there may be a need for someone to advocate for these individuals or groups.

School counselors are in a unique position to serve as an advocate for students. They do not grade or evaluate students' academic performance, and they do not function as disciplinarian for the school. Nor are they in the position of decision-maker regarding school policies that might affect individual students and families.

Further, they may be privy to students' personal concerns, and have the training and background to understand some of the underlying issues and needs of diverse students. Parents and guardians may also feel that the school counselor is more open to discussing their concerns than other school personnel may be.

Being an advocate requires listening carefully. After hearing someone's concerns or identifying an issue, advocacy requires a frank discussion about what kind of help the student or parent/guardian wants. The school counselor needs to assess the appropriateness of the request for this kind of help and determine a good action plan. (See Skills 12.1 and 12.2 for more information about consultation.)

In setting goals to advocate for an individual or a group, the advocate needs to ensure that his or her own personal agenda is not driving the need to speak up. Passion about an issue can be valuable, even necessary at times, to effecting change, but taking action on someone's behalf needs to be grounded in accurately assessing the issues at hand and advocating in a professional manner. A good advocate not only speaks with a strong, compassionate voice but is also able to bring clear thinking, a collaborative attitude, and respectful communication to the table.

ASSESSMENT INSTRUMENTS AND STRATEGIES: OBJECTIVES 0016-0018

OBJECTIVE 0016 *Understand characteristics, uses and limitations of various types of assessment instruments and approaches.*

SKILL 16.1 Major Functions of Appraisal

Assessment can take many forms and serve different purposes. The primary purpose of appraisal is to assist the counselor in helping students recognize their resources, utilize their strengths and accept their limitations, whether the focus is academic, social, personal or vocational. Increasingly, tests are used to measure student performance for reasons other than helping individual students with their educational and career goals. Nonetheless, it is the task of the counselor to assist the student in using all test results for self-understanding and growth.

Formal Assessment Tools

A variety of instruments are used for evaluation purposes. Formal tools with standardized scoring include tests administered by school counselors and other personnel as well as tests administered by the school psychologist. The school psychologist might utilize intelligence tests, which assess the ability to learn, as well as other psychological and aptitude tests in order to determine appropriate placement and develop individualized educational plans when needed.

School counselors, teachers and others may administer achievement tests (which evaluate how much has been learned), tests from the Georgia Student Assessment program measuring student performance, college entrance and preparatory tests (such as SAT, PSAT, and ACT), advanced placement (AP) tests, and others. These tests, while administered at school, are scored offsite by the testing company who prepares and distributes the tests.

Other formal means of appraisal include inventories that measure aptitude, vocational interests, personality traits, and learning styles. Many of these are scored by the school counselor or other personnel administering the test. Counselors may also use assessment tools designed to hone in on behavioral issues such as the incomplete sentence test, lethality inventories, suicide risk assessments, and depression inventories. These need to be used with caution and only with appropriate background and training.

Informal Assessment Tools

School counselors may find they use more informal means of assessment on a more frequent basis. These may involve using some of the inventories mentioned above as discussion tools rather than as formal assessments, behavioral observation of the student in the classroom or other settings, feedback forms developed to evaluate specialized guidance programs, behavior surveys, and needs assessments. The value of all informal assessment tools lies in their ability to give the counselor information that can enhance his or her work with students, and, in many cases, increase the student's self-awareness.

Appraisal can be used for these purposes:

1. To help students recognize and utilize the resources within themselves.

2. To improve self-understanding and to enhance self-concepts.

3. To assess the student's behavior and help the counselor and student anticipate the student's future behavior.

4. To stimulate the student to consider new interests for further exploration and to develop realistic expectations.

5. To provide meaningful information that can help the student make1 intelligent decisions.

6. To aid the counselor and student in identifying and developing future options.

Appraisal also has limitations. These include the following:

1. The use of tests can, at times, interfere with the relationship the counselor has developed with the student, especially if the student is sensitive to being evaluated.

2. There may be a tendency to allow test results to dictate a course of action without considering many other factors. Care needs to be taken not to make assumptions about the student's abilities and choices based on testing alone.

3. If the results of the test are not presented to the student in a manner that promotes self-understanding, more damage than good can result from taking the test.

4. The use of tests tends to put the counselor in the position of an authority, so the student may perceive the test results as the absolute truth.

5. Many informal assessment tools, while helpful in generating discussion, can be used subjectively by both the counselor and the student.

Conditions Affecting Test Results

Testing Room Environment - The comfort of the room and the desk or table and chairs can affect the outcome of the test. The room should be well lighted and ventilated, free of noise and extraneous sound. A minimum distance should be maintained between desks, alternating seats if possible, and the students should be able to hear the directions clearly. The desk should be large enough to provide enough writing space for both the test and the answer sheet

Physical and Mental Condition of the Test Taker - The scores obtained on any test depend to a certain extend on the student's physical and mental condition. Tests should never be scheduled to conflict with other school activities. These would include, but are not limited to, exam week for termination of courses in progress, vacations, and extracurricular activities such as proms and sports events. Students tend to underestimate their physical stamina and do not take into consideration the fact that physical exhaustion impacts mental function.

Related conditions that are beyond the control of the counselor include the stress level of the student, the atmosphere at home, and social interactions students are having with peers that may have erupted immediately before the exam.

Preparation of the Test Taker- This includes both academic preparation (if an achievement test is to be administered) and the preparation given to the student about the mechanics of the test. Motivation to do well on the exam is also an important part of preparation.

Validity of the Test - If the test does not test what it is supposed to test, there is no reason to administer the exam. It is not only a waste of the student's and counselor's time, but it is detrimental to the motivation of the student in sitting for future tests. There is also the added danger of using incorrect and invalid results to determine future goals and placements.

SKILL 16.2   Procedures Involved in Appraisal Administration

Ideally, tests are administered when the student feels the need for additional information for decision making. The parent or other interested parties should not make the decision. If the student makes the decision, motivation is high and this enhances the test accuracy.

Some tests are administered according to the school district's or the state's mandate. These are primarily performance and achievement tests.

When the test materials are received by the administrator of the test, they should be counted and the amount compared to the number on the invoice in order to insure the accuracy of the number of tests received. If possible, they should be placed in a safe with a combination lock known only to a few trusted school personnel. If this is not possible they should be put under locked storage in an area of the school that is not accessible to students and non authorized personnel.

A day or so before the test, the exams should be counted again to confirm that the tests have been kept secure. The tests should be divided according to the room setup and the number of students to be tested. They should then be replaced in the safe location and not taken out until shortly before the test is to be administered. At that time there should be a person in authority present with the tests at all times. Tests should never be left in a room without a proctor. When the students are given a test break, the tests should be closed and the room locked when the students leave.

After the exam is completed the following procedures should be adhered to:

A. Collecting
The proctor should count each exam and answer sheet as it is being collected. If the tests are numbered, each numbered test should be accounted for in order to insure two tests were not given out inadvertently. The students should not leave the room until all the exams and answer sheets are in order.

B. Storing
The tests should be placed in the safe location until it is time for scoring. If the tests are to be returned to the testing company for scoring they should be packaged immediately and prepared for mailing. The service selected for transportation should be notified and a pick-up date should be scheduled as soon as possible. In the meantime the packaged material should be placed in the safe location until picked up for transportation.

C. Safeguarding Data and Testing Instruments
As mentioned, the testing material should be kept confidential at all times until the counselor is released from the responsibility of protecting the tests or when it becomes the responsibility of other professionals. Access to the data results should be available only to authorized personnel. This includes the counselor, the parent/guardian, the student, and possibly a teacher or other school personnel or administrator.

If individuals outside the school community (such as the media or an attorney) want access to the information, permission must be obtained in writing from the student (or parent/guardian if the student is a minor). The information could also be released by a court order if necessary. Legally, the counselor has no authorization to give any information about a student without such permission.

TEACHER CERTIFICATION STUDY GUIDE

OBJECTIVE 0017 *Understand measurement and statistical concepts applicable to individual and group assessment in school settings.*

Skill 17.1 **Knowledge of Measurement Concepts**

The language of testing is unique, and knowledge of interpretation of test data is an important part of the appraisal procedure. Some common terms used in testing and measurement are:

Correlation coefficient - a statistical concept in test validity that measures the relationship between two factors.

Derived score - any score that is not a raw score. It is obtained from a formula that uses the raw score data.

Norming - the scores obtained by a randomly selected group of test takers for the purpose of comparison to future groups of test takers to determine uniform levels of success on the tested information.

Raw Score - the basic score that is usually obtained by counting the number of answers right. It can also be obtained by using the number of answers wrong. The authors of the test can determine any other way to define a raw score. The way the score is defined is noted in the test manual.

Reliability - how dependable or consistent the test is. The three types of reliability are: 1) **scorer reliability:** how consistently different scorers arrive at the same score; often used as a measurement when grading essays or subjective tests; 2) **content reliability**: the degree to which all questions measure the content; 3) **temporal reliability**: how dependable the test is over a long period of time.

Reliability coefficient - a statistical concept in test validity that measures how reliable the relationship is between two factors.

Standard deviation - the specific interval between bands of scores; each interval indicates a different level of achievement.

Standard error of measurement - the inaccuracy of a test caused by chance. Every test has some element of inaccuracy or unreliability so this element of the test is taken into consideration when evaluating the test results. The degree of error is reported in the use of the term standard deviation, which is a band of scores. The formula is this: the square root of 1 minus the reliability coefficient, thus obtaining the standard error of measurement.

Standard score - an indication of the distance between the raw score and the mean of the norm in terms of the standard deviation.

Standardization - Researchers, other than the authors of the test, have provided the protocol to be used to administer the exam, including the provision that the test will be given and scored in the same way at each administration.

Stanine - an interpretation of placement often used in achievement tests. It is a measurement that runs from 1 to 9 and is a band of about one-half a standard deviation in width. Scores are based on percentile values.

Usability - the consideration given to cost, ease of administration, and time taken to score in the administration of the test.

Validity - This is the concept of "does the test, test what it is supposed to test?" In other words, how meaningful is the test? There are four types of validity:

1) **face validity**: Does it look like it may test what it should? (This is not a very dependable source of information.)

2) **content validity**: Is there a close connection between what is taught and what is being tested?

3) **construct validity**: What is the statistical relationship between the scores and another variable that should relate to the test?

4) **empirical validity**: What is the correlation coefficient between the scores and some standard of performance?

TEACHER CERTIFICATION STUDY GUIDE

OBJECTIVE 0018   Understand how to interpret and use assessment to foster individual growth and achievement.

SKILL 18.1   Reporting Assessment Results to Students and Parents

The role of the counselor is not only to supply information to the authorized people concerned with the results of tests, but to be certain the results are interpreted and understood as accurately as possible. The communication of the test results should involve interacting and responding to the feelings and concerns of the student and his/her parent/guardian(s). Test results can be threatening to students and parents. They often feel results are absolutes and reflect a rigid evaluation of the student. Sensitivity to the feelings and needs of the student and the parent are primary in communicating results.

Since counseling is a confidential relationship, the counselor should obtain permission from the student to reveal any information given in confidence. This may sometimes apply to test scores given to parent/guardian(s). At the least, notification to the student that the parent will be receiving the scores and a verbal approval should be obtained.

Once it is clear that the parents are to receive the test report, the counselor should work with the parent in a counseling relationship. Parent/guardian(s) may not react objectively to the child's test results. If they do not agree that the results are consistent with their concept of the child's ability, it may be difficult for them to accept the results. Nevertheless, parents have a right to know, and, to best help their child, need the opportunity to see realistically the abilities of their child. In communicating with the parents, the counselor must be empathetic about the difficulty of accepting new information, and recognize the understanding level of the parent and communicate at that level.

The following techniques of test interpretation are useful in communication.

1.   The interpretation should be related to the goals of the counseling.
All counselor-student relationships are based upon the needs of the student and his/her individuality. Therefore, sharing test data should be framed in this context. The student should be prepared and ready to receive the information and relate it, with the help of the counselor, to the predetermined goals of testing.

2. The results of the test belong to the student.
The goal of testing is to enhance the student's understanding of his/her interests, capabilities, and behavior. The student is entitled to the test results in a timely manner and there should not be a hesitation on the part of the counselor to withhold unfavorable results. Facing the reality of one's abilities is part of the maturation process. This cannot occur if the truth is not communicated or is colored in a manner that could be misinterpreted.

SCHOOL COUNSELING

3. The perception of the student to the scores is of the utmost importance.
If the testing results conflict with self perception, the student could have emotional difficulties in accepting the information. This is where the skill and experience of the counselor comes into play. The goal of the counselor is to help the student and parents accept the information and build upon this new data. The counselor can enhance the likelihood of acceptance by striving to frame the all information (even seemingly negative results) as useful and instructive.

4. Provision should be made for individual interpretation.
It is preferable to interpret test results individually, but often the nature of the test and the number of individuals tested does not lend itself to individual counseling. When group interpretation is required, it is desirable to impress upon the students that individual consultation about their scores is available. In the group setting, the procedure is limited to explaining the purpose of the test and the norm group to which the students have been compared. Individual results should never be announced in the group. Statistics as to what scores are in different stanines or other ranges should be explained so students can evaluate their own results. The counselor should plan on conferring with individual students whose scores are low or whom the counselor knows will be concerned about their scores or when testing is the result of the counseling process.

5. The counselor must be thoroughly familiar with the test.
If the counselor does not understand the significance of the test results, accurate interpretation of the results cannot be expected. Therefore, it is imperative for accuracy as well as credibility purposes that the counselor is thoroughly familiar with the test that has been administered.

6. Interpretation sessions should be structured.
The purpose of structuring is to do away with the mystery of the testing situation, to help the student identify and correct mistaken impressions and to face some realities the results may reveal. Other issues of concern to the student and the parent/guardian(s) should be addressed at another interview, if possible.

7. Test results, not scores, should be communicated at a meaningful level to the student.
The purpose of reporting test results instead of scores is to help students use the information to form more realistic self-concepts. Scores in and of themselves do not impart information about the test taker. The student should understand the implications the results may have for the future. If the student does not understand the information presented, the most accurate information can be useless. Objectivity is the goal of the counselor in presenting the information, so counselor judgments and opinions should not be part of the process. It is also important the counselor explain the language used in the test results, the norming group to which the comparison is being made and the relationship between the score and the present and future goals of the student.

8. The student should help in the interpretation of the results.
This participation allows the counselor to see if the student understands the test results, encourages the student to contribute new information about him/herself into the counseling process, and tends to make the results more acceptable to the student.

9. Test results should, if possible, be verified by other information.
These data could consist of information from others who are familiar with the student as well as information from the students themselves.

10. The counselor, above all, must present the data and results honestly.
If the counselor suspects the student is disappointed with the results, the counselor must make an effort to support the student and explore the student's needs in light of the test results. Additional personal counseling sessions may be in order.

Test results should be retained either for use at another time, for comparison purposes or be made available to parents and others working with the student. Therefore a written record or report should be created. Results must be converted into an understandable form. The language of testing should be reported in the written report to insure consistency in interpretation by all professionals using the data. When a written report is given, it should be presented in a format that is understandable to the person receiving that report; whether it is one highly trained in interpretation, one moderately trained or someone with no training at all. In all cases, dissemination of test results should be on a "need to know" basis and only with the required permission.

There are many ways a written report can be created. These include, but are not limited to, a narrative format delineating the past and present record of the student, a graph form such as horizontal or bar graphs, or as a profile chart.

SKILL 18.2   Sharing and Interpreting Assessment Data

Sharing Data with Other Professionals both Inside and Outside the School

The counselor must make every effort to safeguard this assessment results. School personnel should not have access to such data unless they are directly involved in providing services to the student, such as the school psychologist, special education teacher or school social worker. Generally, a need-to-know basis is the guideline. Under most circumstances, clerical staff, teachers and others should not have access.

While psychotherapists, social workers and other professionals outside the school who are involved with the student are bound by the ethics of confidentiality to which the counselor is bound, this material cannot be released with the express written permission of the student and/or parent/guardian(s). Once a release is obtained, all material relating to the student sent to these people should contain whatever is necessary for the recipient to help the student.

Test scores can be reported directly, as well as the counselor's interpretation of these scores and observations of the student when the scores were presented. This interpretation requires knowledge of the test, its structure and intent, and the scoring guidelines even if the scoring was done offsite. Such information needs to be direct and focused, and should not contain speculation or opinion not based on data. It is particularly important for counselors to be cautious in sharing the results of informal assessment tools.

Interpreting Student Data from Written Reports

The counselor quite often is on the receiving end of written reports about students from various sources. These can be from a reading clinic, a psychiatrist or psychologist, a social worker or a teacher. It is important that the counselor is knowledgeable about the material in the report and, if some of the material is not understandable, investigate further for clarification. If the counselor is to counsel the student based upon these written reports, accuracy in interpretation is essential. Quite often it is appropriate for the counselor to seek a telephone or personal meeting with the writer in order to clarify and consult about the material in the report, as well as collaborate on an action or treatment plan.

OBJECTIVE 0019 *Understand how to plan, administer, and evaluate a comprehensive school guidance and counseling program.*

SKILL 19.1 Components of a Developmental Guidance Program

The ultimate aims of a guidance program include the student's successful acquisition of academic and personal insights in order to make plans for the future with confidence and logic, to obtain personal satisfaction in acquired accomplishments, to make appropriate emotional adjustments, to be able to solve adverse problems as they inevitably occur in life, and to explore vocational and career possibilities intelligently and knowledgeably.

General Guidelines

In order to achieve these goals, a developmental guidance program should be designed and implemented according to the following guidelines:

1. The program must be organized, have established systems of operation, and a stated purpose, along with trained professionals to administer the services.

2. The guidance service must be an accepted and integral part of the school program.

3. The mission statement of the guidance and counseling program should include the promotion of optimum student development and adjustment, with the ultimate goal of developing the child's ability to make intelligent choices and be able to deal with and solve the problems of life.

4. The services to be delivered should include, at a minimum, testing and keeping of appropriate records, personal counseling, the provision of educational and vocational information, appropriate placement into school programs, referrals to outside agencies and professionals, and follow-up of the services provided.

5. The program should provide for identification, exploration and development of the potential inherent in all individuals.

There are many ways to structure the guidance program. The person leading the program should include the staff in making decisions about the type of services to be delivered, the components of those services, and the staff assignment of those components which are consistent with the mission statement of the department. The staff member who is assigned specific duties should have the leeway to decide the components of the service and the method of delivery.

An important part of the success of the guidance program is an informed and supportive school staff, community and student population. The public relations involved in obtaining this support can be time-consuming but ultimately is both rewarding to the counselor and beneficial to students.

The results of the support of those other than the guidance staff in the delivery of guidance services contribute to the optimum functioning of the department and ultimately to the benefit of the students. To promote the guidance department, counselors can do the following:

1. Encourage cooperation between and among the guidance staff, the school staff, the community and the students. A special effort should be made to let teachers and others know that their roles in educating, guiding and counseling all students are vital to the success of the program.

2. Help develop a positive attitude by treating other school colleagues with respect. It may also be helpful to offer workshops and seminars on the functions and specific duties of the guidance staff.

3. Have a well organized program of regular parental contact. This could involve home visits or an advisory committee in which to bounce off solutions to problems, and the discussion and exploration of the feasibility of new programs.

4. Support community projects with a guidance context related to the needs and welfare of children.

5. Solicit the assistance of community leaders to offer mentoring, job shadowing and school-to-work programs.

6. Cooperate in establishing research projects directly related to proven scientific data for the instituting of program decisions and changes.

7. Continuously look for opportunities to promote the guidance program in innovative and unique ways.

Vehicles to Inform Parents/Guardians and Community Members of Guidance Services

Often, parents and guardian as well as other members of the community do not know the extensive functions of the guidance program. Some of the techniques that can be used to inform parents and the community of guidance services and programs are as follows.

1. The guidance newsletter is an excellent vehicle to advertise what is going on in the guidance department and to systematically explain each program on a monthly and ongoing basis.

2. Writing a column in the local newspaper is an effective way to reach community members who do not have students in school.

3. Individual staff members may take turns in speaking to local organizations at their regularly scheduled meetings. These organizations are frequently looking for no-cost speakers to bring members to meetings.

4. Teas and orientations for parents of specific grade level students allow counselors to explain what programs are planned for their students.

5. Participation or attendance at athletic events and other out-of-school functions help counselors become visible to a greater portion of the school population and their parent/guardian(s).

6. When counselors invite community leaders to brainstorm on ways to help students succeed in a chosen field, this increases community awareness of the guidance program. The career night is a good example of this type of activity.

SKILL 19.2 Purposes, Types and Basic Steps in Research, Evaluation and Follow-Up

Purposes of Research

1. **Basic Research** - This is the type of research done for knowledge without a stated practical application. It is often the result of a professional researcher's desire to obtain more knowledge about certain phenomena and is usually done in a clinical or scientific laboratory setting. Application of the results is not considered.

2. **Applied Research** - The techniques used in applied research are the same as those used in basic research. The purpose of the research is in applying the results to the improvement of methods of delivering education to enhance the learning process.

3. **Action Research** - This is the type of research that is directed at a specific problem to be solved. It is done with the immediate goal of applying the results to that specific problem and not done to develop a theory or to create generalizations.

Types of Research

1. **Historical Research** - This type of research is designed to apply the scientific method to describing and analyzing the past, in order to understand the present and perhaps predict the future.

2. **Descriptive Research** - In this work, analysis of the relationships between non-controllable variables and the development of generalizations based on these non-controllable variables is the goal. The formation of generalizations, often used in educational research, can lead to false results as the variables cannot be controlled, human subjects cannot be utilized, and the causes of the problem are often more complicated than the result of a single variable.

    a. Assessment - Is the description given to such types of studies as surveys, polls, activity analysis, and trends. No value judgments, explanation of reasons or causes, or recommendations are given.

    b. Evaluation - Is the value judgment with regard to the effectiveness, desirability or utility of a research project. Some examples of evaluation studies are school surveys (e.g., the student use of drugs) and follow-up studies. Application of findings to solving the particular problem is included in the study without any attempt to generalize.

3. **Experimental and Quasi-Experimental Research** - Is a logical and systematic way of answering the question "If this is done under carefully controlled conditions, what will happen?" This type of research is complicated and does not lend itself easily to the counselor using it in a school setting.

4. **Single Subject Experimental Research** - This type of research focuses upon the individual and not on the results of group experimentation. It is used to test hypotheses of the effect of a particular treatment on one or more behaviors or phenomena.

5. **Qualitative Research** - Focuses upon in-depth interviews, observations, and document analysis. Methods used in this type of holistic educational research include document and content analysis, case studies, and cultural anthropology. This type of research interprets data without the use of numerical analysis.

Basic Steps in Research

All research is based upon the use of the scientific method. This is the attempt to control as many variables of a problem as possible in order to separate out the influences of individual and specific elements of the problem.

1. **Selecting the Research Problem** - The practicing counselor usually has no problem selecting a problem that needs to be solved in the setting in which their work is conducted. The main consideration in the selection of the research problem is determining what can actually be studied. That is, can this variable be observed and measured? Is there an instrument available to measure this variable? If not, can one be designed?

2. **Develop the Research Problem** - The importance of this step in research cannot be too strongly emphasized. Research cannot be conducted on a problem that has not been fully developed. Various parts of the problem should be defined with the help of those familiar with the problem, talking about the problem with colleagues, and thinking about all the aspects of the problem.

Factors, variables and assumptions about the problem that will have an impact on the outcome of the problem should be identified. These variables are an integral part of the research project.

Review of the literature is one of the more important ongoing activities in which the researcher can engage. The reference part of the library contains many sources of information besides scholarly works, to acquaint oneself with what the public feels is important. Incorporating public interest in the project gives the work added benefit.

3. **Formulate the Research Question** - This statement includes all aspects of the question the researcher seeks to answer. It is specific in defining the population involved, gives a general description of the situation under which the research will be conducted, and always states the comparison group or groups to be compared. It is posed in the form of a question.

    a. Purpose statement - This statement tells what the study intends to do and how it will aid the researcher in answering the question(s) posed. In proposals, this statement is written in the present tense; in completed research this statement is written in the past tense.

    b. Procedural statement - This statement follows naturally from the purpose statement. It tells the reader what actions were taken to gain the results of the study.

c. Hypotheses - This is the statement of what the researcher believes will be the relationship between the variables. The *research hypothesis* is what the researcher believes will be found as a result of the research. The *null hypothesis* is the statistical and logical opposite of the research hypothesis. Since we cannot often predict what will happen, we can often predict what will not happen. This is the purpose of the null hypotheses. The *alternative hypothesis* is a statement of the possibility of other variables not specifically addressed in the design.

4. **Organize the Plan for the Research Report** - The research report has the following components:
    a. Introduction
    b. Hypothesis
    c. Review of the Literature
    d. Method (research design) used in conducting the research
    e. Results
    f. Conclusions
    g. Discussion
    h. References

Basic Steps in Evaluation and Follow-Up

The evaluation of the research should be done by an unbiased party due to the critical nature of the evaluation. Some of the following questions should be asked in the critique. Does the title of the research clearly reflect the research done? Is the problem and hypothesis clearly defined and testable? Are terms defined? Is the related literature summarized adequately, relative to the problem, is it well organized, and are important findings emphasized? Is the design described adequately, are variables and samples described, are controls and data gathering instruments and procedures appropriate, and can the research be replicated? Do the results of the research use appropriate statistics, tables, and charts, and is the analysis of the relationship of the data logical and objective? Finally, is the discussion of the research clear and objective, and are the findings justified by the data presented?

The follow-up procedure is done after the program has been in effect for an established period of time. Longitudinal studies can be done to see if the program established by the research is still effective after a period of time; a survey instrument can be used in follow-up studies to ascertain if the participants felt there was a significant change from before the study, and to see if the results of the program established from the research study are relatively permanent in nature.

Interpretation of Results of Research, Evaluation and Follow-Up
In the discussion portion of any research project, the level of significance of the study is reported by the researcher. This is most often used in determining the effectiveness of the research with evaluation and follow-up of the procedures used. The attainment of statistical significance (usually reported as 0.05 or less, meaning the results were unlikely to be due to chance) is not always the determining factor of the worth of a program. The evaluator of the program must interpret what the results mean, the influence of the variables on those results and the relation of each statistical analysis to the hypothesis formulated at the beginning of the study.

Practical significance is another criterion for judging the contribution of the study to every day practice. Implications for possible change derived from the practical application of the results may be valuable for the improvement of the program. Shortcomings in the research may become clear; in this case additional research should be considered.

SKILL 19.3   Needs Assessment and Program Evaluation Techniques

Needs Assessment - The needs assessment is an extensive preliminary study of the real and perceived wants and requirements of a population, community or group. A series of complete and extensive questions are formulated to be submitted to all facets of the population involved. The design of the needs assessment study should be carefully formulated so the results can be analyzed in relation to the purpose of the study.

For example, a needs assessment of a school community would consist of community taxpayers, community leaders, parents, school administrators, teachers, support staff and students. Other individuals may come forward who wish to participate in the study and they should be included if they have a connection with the purpose of the study.

Program Evaluation Techniques - Program evaluation is often a requirement of funding sources or of administrators. Some there is a sincere wish to see if a program is producing the desired results; other times the demand for an evaluation is the result of political pressure, to either discredit opponents of the program or to strengthen their own positions on the value of the program. Finances influence the requirement of a program evaluation for a variety of reasons.

There are two broad types of program evaluation: formative and summative.

Formative Evaluation - This type of evaluation involves the collection of data while a program is in the *developmental, implementational,* or *operational* stage. In the *developmental* stage the evaluator tries to determine the general goals, the specific outcomes or behaviors to be attained, and the current performance level of the population of the program to be evaluated. In the *implementational* stage the evaluator tries to determine if the program is implemented appropriately and the identified population is participating in the program. In the *operational* stage the evaluator looks at how well the program is running. Other information to gather is finding out if the staff is adequate and well trained and if any unanticipated difficulties have surfaced.

Summative Evaluation - This type of evaluation involves the collection of data after a program has been in place for a period of time. The summative evaluation is often done after one year of operation. This may not be an adequate amount of time to determine the effectiveness of the program, depending on the nature of the program. The summative evaluation often is used to determine if the program will be continued.

Models used in evaluation can be classified in the following manner.

The **CIPP Model** has four stages. *Context evaluation* identifies the elements of a setting and the discrepancies between what exists and what is desirable. *Input evaluation* is the analysis of available resources and methods for the selection of the most appropriate course of action. *Process evaluation* is the collection of data about the progress of the program. *Product evaluation* is the process of determining the extent to which the program has achieved its goals. In this model the evaluator gathers the information needed to make a decision in each stage and presents this material to the administrator for decision making.

Discrepancy Evaluation - The evaluator compares the degree of agreement between program standards and program performance. *Program standards* are the criteria the developers of the program identified for utilization of resources, procedural operations, program management and final outcomes. *Program performance* is what actually occurred when the program was operational in the educational setting. The five questions the evaluator answers are:

> Are standards defined in measurable terms?
> Are behavioral objectives stated clearly?
> What instruments are developed or selected to measure the standards?
> What data has been collected on performance?
> Has the data been used to determine the discrepancy between standards and performance?

The findings of the evaluator are then submitted in a report.

Adversarial Evaluation - The evaluator and administrator, with the help of the personnel involved in the program, compile a list of issues to evaluate. Issues are selected that are determined to be the most important to the success of the program. Selected personnel form teams to either support or oppose the program, gathering information to support their stand and prepare arguments for their side of the issues. The teams present their arguments before a panel of decision makers who make the final decision as to the modification, elimination or retention of the program.

SKILL 19.4 New Programming: Developing Objectives and Determining Outcomes Based on Data

New and innovative programs and methods are sometimes introduced without careful consideration of their value for the setting in which they are to be used. The school counselor should assess new programs before implementing them.

Factors to consider are:

- Will this program be acceptable to the community?
- What will be the cost to the school district?
- Can grant money be obtained to initiate the program?
- Will that money be available on a continuous basis or will it run out after a period of time?

A needs assessment of the school community might be in order to see if the program is acceptable. As an example, the health department might feel a program of smoking cessation would be beneficial to the students. In a needs assessment survey, students might feel that smoking is a desired activity on their part and so they would not attend this type of activity. It might be more advantageous to the health department to develop a unit on the health damage smoking causes to the individual in later life.

Before adding a program to the guidance and counseling curriculum, how this task will be accomplished should be evaluated. Will new staff be needed or will this program fall to the existing staff? If the latter is the case, will other programs now in existence have less time allotted or can some ineffective program now be eliminated? Can the staff view the suggested new program in operation in another school? If this can be done, the counselors in the other school should be questioned as to the strengths and weaknesses of the program, how they would change the program, and what benefits have the students experienced by instituting this program.

Program objectives should be developed before the adoption of any program. These objectives are based upon the needs of the population to be served and can be drawn from the needs assessment. Program objectives should be written with measurable goals and a clear methodology for evaluating the achievement or lack of achievement of the goals.

After all evaluative data have been compiled and analyzed, the person in charge of the program determines the degree to which program objectives have been obtained. If the formulation of the program objectives was done carefully and there is indisputable evidence that these objectives have not been reached, it is ethical to eliminate the program and start again from scratch. If there is an undeniable opinion that the program objectives have been obtained, then the retention of the program and further plans for expansion should be the result.

Problems can arise when there is no clear evidence of attainment of program objectives, or if some of the objectives have been attained but others, considered more important, have not been accomplished. It is clear that modification of the program is in order. The task of rebuilding the methods in order to reach the stated objectives should begin with a new perspective of what needs to be done to improve the program. Perhaps people who have not had initial input into the program should be recruited to help in the revision of the program. Perhaps the original objectives of the program were unrealistic. These can be difficult questions to resolve and require thought and effort.

OBJECTIVE 0020 Understand roles, responsibilities, and professional standards of school counselors

SKILL 20.1 Professional Standards of the American Counseling Association (ACA) and the American School Counseling Association (ASCA)

The ACA Code of Ethics and Standards of Practice were first developed in 1961 and revised in 1974. Since then they were revised approximately every seven years, the latest revision being in 2005. These codes are detailed below.

The Counseling Relationship
The relationship between counselors and clients is based on trust and respect. Therefore, counselor is responsible for respecting the dignity of all clients and always being mindful of the clients' welfare. The counselor must keep appropriate records, get informed consent, maintain professional boundaries, be culturally and developmentally competent, and be ever vigilant about avoiding harm to clients.

Confidentiality
It is important the counselors provide their services in a culturally competence manner that respects the rights of the client. Clients must be provided with information and guidelines by which the counselor may breech confidentiality. This informed consent may need to be reviewed throughout the counseling relationship. Records containing sensitive information about clients should be handled with the great care and discretion in location. Exceptions of confidentiality may include when clients are in danger of harming themselves or someone else and when the counselor's work with the client is court-ordered, with disclosure being a condition of the counseling. At all times, the counselor must make every effort to protect the information the client has disclosed within the confines of the trust-based relationship.

Professional Responsibility
Counselors must have a working knowledge of their ethical responsibilities as they work with clients. To best serve their clients, counselors need to know the extent of their competence (knowing when to refer a client to another provider), be involved with continued professional development, clearly and realistically publicize their services, fairly represent their professional qualifications, monitor the effectiveness of services rendered, and rigorously practice codes of conduct that are nondiscriminatory.

Relationships with other Professionals
Consultation is a powerful tool in the counseling practice. No counselor is expected nor should be expected to know how to work with all populations, cases, and presenting challenges. Establishing relationships with other professionals and specialists allows counselors to discuss the effectiveness of case management, maintain confidentiality, and to increase overall effectiveness of the services provided to the client.

Evaluation, Assessment, and Interpretation
Assessments may be related to education, career or psychological issues. Intended use of any instrument must be disclosed to the client. Multicultural considerations are taken into account to avoid assessments that are inappropriate due to a biased empirical background. Part of counselors' continued professional development is to ensure that any assessment used is the most recent version available. Legal proceedings for forensic evaluations can include that of the professional opinion of the counselor as well as written or court-ordered consent.

Teaching, Training, and Supervision
Consultation with professionals allows supervising counselors to ethically monitor the work of counselors-in-training. Before serving as a supervisor, counselors undergo extensive training in policy and procedures in the areas of appraisal and evaluation. Supervisors have an ethical obligation to the clients of the supervisee to ensure the services provided are appropriate. Supervisors need to encourage counselors-in-training to refrain from providing counseling and related services when their physical, mental and emotional well-being are called in to question.

Research and Publications
It is imperative that counselors establish and maintain ethical standards in conducting research. Participants must be notified of the purpose of the study, and how their input or results will be used, as well as receive information about the results of the overall project. Federal and state laws as well as institutional regulations need to be firmly adhered to.

Resolving Ethical Issues
Following ethical and professional standards is critical to the importance of the work counselors do with their clients. Ethical standards not only prevent harm to the client, but also protect the counselor from making unfounded and unintentional mistakes. Counselors need to consult with other counseling professionals about any situation or case that warrants an ethical question or decision. Should a counselor suspect a colleague of ethical misconduct, ACA expects counselors to follow the protocol as illustrated in the ACA Policy and Procedures for Processing Complaints of Ethical Violations.

These eight topics cover the most often questioned areas of ethical practice. They are by no means all inclusive; instead they are guidelines as to basic ethical behavior. Although the ethics guidelines are more specific than standards of practice, they cannot possibly include all situations. Standards of practice are, by their nature, more generic and provide basic behavior standards for all counselors. These codes serve the purpose of identifying areas of concern, not of providing a "cook book recipe" as to standards of conduct or as to the resolution of specific ethical situations.

When an issue of ethics arises in the counselor's practice in any context (i.e., private practice, a school setting or an agency) it is wise to have one's own process of determining the course of action. Reference to the ACA Code of Ethics would be the first step in the resolution of the problem. Additionally, after formulating a course of action, all the ramifications of that course of action should be weighed. If there are any doubts as to the ethics of this course of action, colleagues, attorneys and specialists should be consulted.

In the past, divisions of ACA, such as ASCA, had their own code of ethics, but in 1997, with the revision of the code, divisions were asked to dissolve their codes and develop Best Practice Guidelines as a basic coverage with specific codes that apply to their specialty areas. To review ASCA standards, go to www.schoolcounselor.org/content.asp?contentid=173.

To view ACA's Code of Ethics or access resources related to ethical dilemmas, go to www.counseling.org/Resources/CodeOfEthics/TP/Home/CT2.aspx.

SKILL 20.2   Professional Development

Licensure

Professional counselors can be certified in different areas by the National Board of Certified Counselors (NBCC) (www.nbcc.org), as well as licensed by the state of Georgia (sos.georgia.gov/plb/counselors/) These certifying agents have their own codes of ethics to which members are accountable. The counselor who holds each specific certification or license is ethically bound and accountable to know and abide by their ethical code. Violations can and should be reported to these monitoring agencies for potential consequences to the counselor.

Continuing Education

All licensing and certifying bodies require a requisite number of hours of continuing education. Regardless, all school counselors have a professional and ethical responsibility to stay abreast of current developments in the field. Attending conferences and seminars can provide professional nourishment and also be helpful in preventing burnout in what can be a very demanding career. In addition to going to programs geared specifically to school counseling and guidance, counselors may find it interesting and helpful to participate in workshops and training programs designed for mental health professionals, educators, social workers, and administrators. Attending meetings of the local, state and national counselor associations can also be informative.

Go to www.schoolcounselor.org/content.asp?pl=325&sl=129&contentid=129 for more information about professional development opportunities, including the Georgia state conference.

OBJECTIVE 0021 *Understand legal and ethical issues related to the rights and responsibilities of students, parents/guardians and school personnel.*

SKILL 21.1 Legal Rights of Students and Parents Concerning Student Records and Assessment Data

School employees, on a need-to-know basis, may have access to student records. These individuals may include principals, assistant principals, school psychologists, school counselors, and special education professionals. Regardless of his or her position, each employee must maintain the confidentiality of student information.

In 1973, Congress passed a federal statute called FERPA to clarify the legal rights of students and parent/guardian(s) concerning access to student records. Also known as the "Buckley Amendment, FERPA stands for Family Educational Rights and Privacy Act (20 U.S.C. § 1232g; 34 CFR Part 99). (Go to nces.ed.gov/forum/FERPA_links.asp for more information about FERPA.)

Schools that receive funds from the federal government must comply with FERPA. The rights afforded by FERPA apply to parent/guardian(s) of students under the age of eighteen. Once a student turns eighteen, these rights are then transferred to the "eligible" student.

Under 34 CFR Part 99.7, FERPA states that parent/guardian(s) be notified on an annual basis about their rights to have access to or review their student's records. The following criteria must be included in the annual notification:

1. Parent/guardian(s) have the right to review their child's records
2. Parent/guardian(s) can advocate for changes to be made to the record should any information be incorrect.
3. Parent/guardian(s) can provide or withhold consent for the disclosure of personal information located with their child's record.
4. The way in which a parent/guardian can file a complaint with the Department of Education concerning a school or institution's failure to comply with FERPA.
5. Define which school officials that may have access to school records.

Schools may use a variety of ways to inform parents about their rights such as the school or community newspaper, bulletin boards, and student handbooks. Schools are not required to individually inform parents of their rights. Schools must procure parental consent to share student personal information. For example, a high school counselor must have a consent form on file before providing information to a college concerning a student's academic background. The ethical counselor will with hold providing personal information (except for information that has been published publicly, such as a student directory) to colleges, military recruiters, and coaches without gaining consent of the parent or guardian.

All assessment data are considered student records and must be kept confidential. Legally and ethically, only the students and/or their parent/guardian(s) have the right to access unless they have specifically signed a waiver or requested that the information be shared with colleges, outside professionals, or other personnel such as attorneys.

A good resource for issues related to student privacy and confidentiality can be found at nces.ed.gov/pubs2006/stu_privacy/intro.asp.

SKILL 21.2 Knowledge of Use of Legislation in Regards to Special Needs Students

Special education law is filled with abbreviations. In the following explanations the abbreviations are used instead of the actual names of the acts or authorities. The following is a list of these abbreviations for easy reference. (See www.ed.gov for more information.)

EDGAR - Education Department General Administrative Regulations

EAHCA - Education for all Handicapped Children Act

EHA - Education for the Handicapped Act

FAPE - Free Appropriate Public Education

IEP - Individualized Education Program

IFSP - Individualized Family Service Plan

IDEA - Individuals with Disabilities Act

ITDA - Infants and Toddlers with Disabilities Act

LEA - Local Education Authority

OCR - Office of Civil Rights (U.S. Department of Education).

OSERS - Office of Special Education and Rehabilitative Services (U.S. Department of Education)

OSEP - Office of Special Education Programs (U.S. Department of Education)

SEA - State Education Authority

In 1975 Congress signed into law the Individuals with Disabilities Education Act (IDEA), or Public Law 94-142, making local and state education entities responsible for providing children with disabilities a "free and appropriate public education." This act was a turning point in the education of children with disabilities providing that these children have a right to FAPE and also provided for procedural protections to insure that they received this FAPE. Subsequently Section 504 of the Rehabilitation Act of 1993 was enacted and also affected educational rights of children with disabilities.

There are overlapping provisions as well as differences between these laws with Section 504 being broad and general, including a wider range of discrimination while IDEA is more specific and detailed. Other Acts delineate the delivery procedures of education services to children with disabilities.

Brown vs. Board of Education and Mills vs. Board of Education were two important legal decisions that helped hasten the enactment of education protections for children with disabilities. Section 504 of the Rehabilitation Act of 1993 provided that "No otherwise qualified handicapped individual ... shall solely by reason of his handicap be excluded from participation, in, be denied the benefits of, or be subjected to discrimination under any program or activity receiving federal assistance." The subsequent amendments provided for payment of costs of attorney's fees and damages to parents if they proved successful in legal suits brought against educational institutions for not providing their children with a FAPE.

IDEA is a funding vehicle of the Federal Government for a SEA to provide a FAPE to all children with disabilities. In addition if a state opts to provide a FAPE for children ages three to five and eighteen to twenty one, it must, under IDEA, provide that opportunity for all children with disabilities in those age groups. In addition if any children <u>without</u> disabilities in those age groups are provided with educational services, then a proportionate share of those with disabilities must also be provided with that educational service. The funding is provided by a complicated formula taking into account the number of children in a given state who have been classified as disabled.

Each state monitors the devising and implementing its own FAPE. The main provision enacted by Congress was the requirement that each child classified be provided with an IEP on an annual basis. Procedural protections include that the child be identified, evaluated by a multi-disciplinary team, eligibility for special education determined, and an IEP developed with parental participation.

SKILL 21.3 Laws Regarding Child Abuse and Neglect

Every state, including Georgia, has laws that require the reporting of suspected abuse and neglect of children under the age of 18. The counselor should investigate the state laws as well as the policies of the school district in which he or she will be working in order to become familiar with the procedures to follow in reporting suspected cases.

Although the confidentiality of the counselor/client relationship may be violated, the school counselor has a duty to protect the minor child from harm. Most often, though, the child who is a victim of such abuse, and who reports it to the counselor, is seeking help. The skillful counselor seeks the consent of the child to report the incident or incidents in an effort to maintain a trusting relationship with the child.

Detailed below is the law in Georgia requiring the reporting of suspected child abuse and neglect. It is taken from the Official Code of Georgia Annotated (2007).

O.C.G.A. § 19-7-5 (2007)

§ 19-7-5. Reporting of child abuse; when mandated or authorized; content of report; to whom made; immunity from liability; report based upon privileged communication; penalty for failure to report

(a) The purpose of this Code section is to provide for the protection of children whose health and welfare are adversely affected and further threatened by the conduct of those responsible for their care and protection. It is intended that the mandatory reporting of such cases will cause the protective services of the state to be brought to bear on the situation in an effort to prevent further abuses, to protect and enhance the welfare of these children, and to preserve family life wherever possible. This Code section shall be liberally construed so as to carry out the purposes thereof.

(b) As used in this Code section, the term:

(1) "Abused" means subjected to child abuse.

(2) "Child" means any person under 18 years of age.

(3) "Child abuse" means:

(A) Physical injury or death inflicted upon a child by a parent or caretaker thereof by other than accidental means; provided, however, physical forms of discipline may be used as long as there is no physical injury to the child;

    (B) Neglect or exploitation of a child by a parent or caretaker thereof;

    (C) Sexual abuse of a child; or

    (D) Sexual exploitation of a child.

However, no child who in good faith is being treated solely by spiritual means through prayer in accordance with the tenets and practices of a recognized church or religious denomination by a duly accredited practitioner thereof shall, for that reason alone, be considered to be an "abused" child.

  (3.1) "Sexual abuse" means a person's employing, using, persuading, inducing, enticing, or coercing any minor who is not that person's spouse to engage in any act which involves:

    (A) Sexual intercourse, including genital-genital, oral-genital, anal-genital, or oral-anal, whether between persons of the same or opposite sex;

    (B) Bestiality;

    (C) Masturbation;

    (D) Lewd exhibition of the genitals or pubic area of any person;

    (E) Flagellation or torture by or upon a person who is nude;

    (F) Condition of being fettered, bound, or otherwise physically restrained on the part of a person who is nude;

    (G) Physical contact in an act of apparent sexual stimulation or gratification with any person's clothed or unclothed genitals, pubic area, or buttocks or with a female's clothed or unclothed breasts;

    (H) Defecation or urination for the purpose of sexual stimulation; or

    (I) Penetration of the vagina or rectum by any object except when done as part of a recognized medical procedure.

"Sexual abuse" shall not include consensual sex acts involving persons of the opposite sex when the sex acts are between minors or between a minor and an adult who is not more than five years older than the minor. This provision shall not be deemed or construed to repeal any law concerning the age or capacity to consent.

  (4) "Sexual exploitation" means conduct by a child's parent or caretaker who allows, permits, encourages, or requires that child to engage in:

    (A) Prostitution, as defined in Code Section 16-6-9; or

    (B) Sexually explicit conduct for the purpose of producing any visual or print medium depicting such conduct, as defined in Code Section 16-12-100.

  (c)(1) The following persons having reasonable cause to believe that a child has been abused shall report or cause reports of that abuse to be made as provided in this Code section:

(A) Physicians licensed to practice medicine, interns, or residents;

(B) Hospital or medical personnel;

(C) Dentists;

(D) Licensed psychologists and persons participating in internships to obtain licensing pursuant to Chapter 39 of Title 43;

(E) Podiatrists;

(F) Registered professional nurses or licensed practical nurses licensed pursuant to Chapter 24 of Title 43;

(G) Professional counselors, social workers, or marriage and family therapists licensed pursuant to Chapter 10A of Title 43;

(H) School teachers;

(I) School administrators;

(J) School guidance counselors, visiting teachers, school social workers, or school psychologists certified pursuant to Chapter 2 of Title 20;

(K) Child welfare agency personnel, as that agency is defined pursuant to Code Section 49-5-12;

(L) Child-counseling personnel;

(M) Child service organization personnel; or

(N) Law enforcement personnel.

(2) If a person is required to report abuse pursuant to this subsection because that person attends to a child pursuant to such person's duties as a member of the staff of a hospital, school, social agency, or similar facility, that person shall notify the person in charge of the facility, or the designated delegate thereof, and the person so notified shall report or cause a report to be made in accordance with this Code section. A staff member who makes a report to the person designated pursuant to this paragraph shall be deemed to have fully complied with this subsection. Under no circumstances shall any person in charge of such hospital, school, agency, or facility, or the designated delegate thereof, to whom such notification has been made exercise any control, restraint, modification, or make other change to the information provided by the reporter, although each of the aforementioned persons may be consulted prior to the making of a report and may provide any additional, relevant, and necessary information when making the report.

(d) Any other person, other than one specified in subsection (c) of this Code section, who has reasonable cause to believe that a child is abused may report or cause reports to be made as provided in this Code section.

(e) An oral report shall be made immediately, but in no case later than 24 hours from the time there is reasonable cause to believe a child has been abused, by telephone or otherwise and followed by a report in writing, if requested, to a child welfare agency providing protective services, as designated by the Department of Human Resources, or, in the absence of such agency, to an appropriate police authority or district attorney. If a report of child abuse is made to the child welfare agency or independently discovered by the agency, and the agency has reasonable cause to believe such report is true or the report contains any allegation or evidence of child abuse, then the agency shall immediately notify the appropriate police authority or district attorney. Such reports shall contain the names and addresses of the child and the child's parents or caretakers, if known, the child's age, the nature and extent of the child's injuries, including any evidence of previous injuries, and any other information that the reporting person believes might be helpful in establishing the cause of the injuries and the identity of the perpetrator. Photographs of the child's injuries to be used as documentation in support of allegations by hospital staff, physicians, law enforcement personnel, school officials, or staff of legally mandated public or private child protective agencies may be taken without the permission of the child's parent or guardian. Such photograph shall be made available as soon as possible to the chief welfare agency providing protective services and to the appropriate police authority.

(f) Any person or persons, partnership, firm, corporation, association, hospital, or other entity participating in the making of a report or causing a report to be made to a child welfare agency providing protective services or to an appropriate police authority pursuant to this Code section or any other law or participating in any judicial proceeding or any other proceeding resulting therefrom shall in so doing be immune from any civil or criminal liability that might otherwise be incurred or imposed, provided such participation pursuant to this Code section or any other law is made in good faith. Any person making a report, whether required by this Code section or not, shall be immune from liability as provided in this subsection.

(g) Suspected child abuse which is required to be reported by any person pursuant to this Code section shall be reported notwithstanding that the reasonable cause to believe such abuse has occurred or is occurring is based in whole or in part upon any communication to that person which is otherwise made privileged or confidential by law.

(h) Any person or official required by subsection (c) of this Code section to report a suspected case of child abuse who knowingly and willfully fails to do so shall be guilty of a misdemeanor.

(i) A report of child abuse or information relating thereto and contained in such report, when provided to a law enforcement agency or district attorney pursuant to subsection (e) of this Code section or pursuant to Code Section 49-5-41, shall not be subject to public inspection under Article 4 of Chapter 18 of Title 50 even though such report or information is contained in or part of closed records compiled for law enforcement or prosecution purposes unless:

(1) There is a criminal or civil court proceeding which has been initiated based in whole or in part upon the facts regarding abuse which are alleged in the child abuse reports and the person or entity seeking to inspect such records provides clear and convincing evidence of such proceeding; or

(2) The superior court in the county in which is located the office of the law enforcement agency or district attorney which compiled the records containing such reports, after application for inspection and a hearing on the issue, shall permit inspection of such records by or release of information from such records to individuals or entities who are engaged in legitimate research for educational, scientific, or public purposes and who comply with the provisions of this paragraph. When those records are located in more than one county, the application may be made to the superior court of any one of such counties. A copy of any application authorized by this paragraph shall be served on the office of the law enforcement agency or district attorney which compiled the records containing such reports. In cases where the location of the records is unknown to the applicant, the application may be made to the Superior Court of Fulton County. The superior court to which an application is made shall not grant the application unless:

(A) The application includes a description of the proposed research project, including a specific statement of the information required, the purpose for which the project requires that information, and a methodology to assure the information is not arbitrarily sought;

(B) The applicant carries the burden of showing the legitimacy of the research project; and

(C) Names and addresses of individuals, other than officials, employees, or agents of agencies receiving or investigating a report of abuse which is the subject of a report, shall be deleted from any information released pursuant to this subsection unless the court determines that having the names and addresses open for review is essential to the research and the child, through his or her representative, gives permission to release the information.

TEACHER CERTIFICATION STUDY GUIDE

OBJECTIVE 0022 *Understand applications of current and emerging technology in education and In the professional practice of school counselors.*

Skill 22.1   Using Technology Effectively

The core of a school counselor's job involves communication and connection with students, parents/guardians, teachers, administrators, other school personnel and outside professionals. The personal relationship between counselors and others cannot be supplanted by technology. However, since communication and information are central to a school counselor's work, technology can be utilized very effectively to enhance the school counselor's functioning.

There are several areas in which school counselors need to be technologically proficient. One is in basic computer skills, such as keyboarding, word processing, and using email. Many schools have computerized much student data and scheduling, and therefore school counselors must be able to access and utilize this information efficiently. Email is also a primary form of communication in many school districts, and counselors, like all faculty and staff, must be able to communicate using this format.

Increasingly, parents and guardians are also using email to communicate with school personnel. Some school districts have created specific interactive programs on the school's website to facilitate the sharing of information with parents, guardians, community members, teachers and other school personnel.

A second area in which school counselors are increasingly required to be technologically savvy is in the use of the internet to access information. While there are many types of internet information that may be relevant to school counselors' work, of particular importance is information about career development, higher education, training programs, and financial aid. Students and many parents/guardians utilize the internet as their primary source for gathering data, and counselors must be able to interact intelligently with and even guide students in their search for information. This requires not only a facility in using internet browsers and search engines, but the capacity to assess the value and utility of different websites.

Thirdly, counselors need to be able to use software to develop presentations and graphics for the classroom, at conferences or meetings, for reports, and with colleagues. Most professional fields require such capacity and school counselors need to stay current with the opportunities offered by technology. This may also involve a working knowledge of hardware used for presentations.

SCHOOL COUNSELING

BIBLIOGRAPHY

BEST, J.W. & KAHN, J.V., (1996), *Research in Education,* 7th Edition. Boston: Allyn & Bacon, Inc.

BRAGSTAD, B.J., & STUMPF, S. M., (1987), *A Guidebook for Teaching Study Skills and Motivation,* 2nd Edition, Boston: Allyn & Bacon, Inc.

BROWNELL, J., (1986), *Building Active Listening Skills,* Englewood Cliffs, NJ: Prentice-Hall Inc.

BUKSTEIN, O.G., (1995), *Substance Abuse - Adolescent Assessment & Prevention,* John Wiley & Sons.

BURLEY-ALLEN, M., (1982), *Listening: The Forgotten Skill,* Hoboken, NJ: John Wiley & Sons, Inc.

CARTWRIGNT, D., & ZANDER, A., Editors, (1968), *Group Dynamics, Research & Theory,* 3rd Edition, New York: Harper & Row.

CATES, W.M., (1985), *A Practical Guide to Educational Research,* Englewood Cliffs, NJ: Prentice-Hall Inc.

COREY, G., (1991), *Manual For Theory & Practice of Counseling & Psychotherapy,* 4th Edition, Pacific Grove, CA: Brooks/Cole Publishing Co.

COREY, G., (1996), *Instructor's Manual for Theory & Practice of Counseling & Psychotherapy,* 5th Edition, Pacific Grove, CA: Brooks/Cole Publishing Co.

COREY, G., (1996), *Student Manual for Theory & Practice of Counseling & Psychotherapy,* 5th Edition, Pacific Grove, CA:, Brooks/Cole Publishing Co.

COREY, G., (1990), *Theory & Practice of Group Counseling,* 3rd Edition, Pacific Grove, CA: Brooks/Cole Publishing Co.

COTTLE, W.C., (1968), *Guidance Monograph Series, Series 111, Testing, Interest & Personality Inventories,* Boston: Houghton Mifflin Co.

DOUGHERTY, A.M., (1995), *Case Studies in Human Services Consultation,* Pacific Grove, CA: Brooks/Cole Publishing Co.

DOWNING, L.N., (1968), *Guidance & Counseling Services, An Introduction,* New York, McGraw-Hill Book Co.

DRESHMAN, J.L., CRABBE, C.L. & TARASEVICH, S. (2001), *Caring in Times of Crisis: A Crisis Management/Postvention Manual for Administrators, Student Assistance Teams & Other School Personnel K-12.* Chapin, SC: Youthlight, Inc.

DUNN, R. & DUNN, K., (1978), *Teaching Students through Their Individual Learning Styles, A Practical Approach,* Reston, VA: Reston Publishing Co.

ERIKSON, E.H., (1963), *Childhood & Society,* 2nd Edition, New York, W.W. Norton & Co. Inc.

GOLDMAN, L., (1961), *Century Psychology Series, Using Tests in Counseling,* New York, Appleton-Century Crofts.

GRESSARD, C.F., & KEEL, L. *Counseling Today,* February 1998, *Ethics in Counseling,* pg. 16.

GUERNSEY, T.F. & KLARE, K., (1993), *Special Education Law,* Durham, NC: Carolina Academic Press.

HAZLER, R.J., PH.D., (1996), *Breaking the Cycle of Violence,* Washington, DC: Accelerated Development.

HERGENHAHN B.R., (1988), *An Introduction to Theories of Learning,* 3rd Edition, Englewood Cliffs, NJ: Prentice-Hall Inc.

JOHNSON, D.W., JOHNSON, R.T., (1995), *Reducing School Violence through Conflict Resolution,* Alexandria, VA: Association for Supervision & Curriculum Development.

JOHNSON, D.W., & JOHNSON, F.P., (1975), *Joining Together, Group Theory & Group Skills,* Englewood Cliffs, NJ: Prentice-Hall Inc.

KEMP, C.G., (1964), *Perspectives on the Group Process,* Boston, Houghton Mifflin Co.

LYMAN, H.B., (1968), *Guidance Monograph Series, Series 111 Testing, Intelligence, Aptitude & Achievement Testing,* Boston: Houghton Mifflin Co.

MAHLER, C., CALDWELL, E., (1961), *Group Counseling in Secondary Schools,* Chicago, IL: Science Research Associates.

MAHLER, C., (1969). *Group Counseling in the School.* Boston: Houghton Mifflin Co.

MEYERING R.A., (1968), *Guidance Monograph Series,, Series 11 Counseling, Use of Test Data in Counseling,* Boston: Houghton Mifflin Co.

MCDANIELS, C., NORMAN, C.G., (1992), *Counseling for Career Development,* 1st Edition, San Francisco: Jossey-Bass Publishers.

Forum Guide to the Privacy of Student Information: A Resource for Schools (NFES 2006–805). (2006). U.S. Dept of Education. Washington, DC: National Center for Education Statistics.

OSIPOW, S.H., (1968), *Theories of Career Development,* New York, Century Psychology Series, Appleton-Century Crofts, Educational Division of Meredith Corp.

OSIPOW, S.H., FITZGERALD, L.F., (1996), *Theories of Career Development,* 4th Edition, Boston: Allyn & Bacon.

OSIPOW, S.H., & WALSH, W.B., (1970), *Strategies in Counseling for Behavior Change,* New York: Century Psychology Series, Appleton-Century Crofts.

PATTERSON, C.H., (1966), *Theories of Counseling & Psychotherapy,* New York, Harper-Row.

REEVES, E.T., (1970), *The Dynamics of Group Behavior,* New York: American Management Association, Inc.

ROGERS, D., (1969), *Readings in Child Psychology,* Pacific Groves, CA: Brooks/Cole Publishing Co.

SHAW, M.E., (1976), *Group Dynamics - The Psychology of Small Group Behavior,* 2nd Edition, New York: McGraw-Hill Book Co.

SIMS, R.R., & SIMS, S.J., (1995), *The Importance of Learning Styles,* Westport, CT: Greenwood Press.

VANDRACEK, R.M., LERNER, M.R., & SCHULENBERG, J.E., (1986), *Career Development: A Life Span Developmental Approach,* Hillsdale, NJ: Lawrence Erlbaum Associates.

WHITE, J., MULLIS, F., EARLEG, B., & BRIGMAN, G., (1995), *Consultation in Schools, The Counselors Role,* Portland, ME: J. Weston Walch.

YALOM, I.D. & LESZCZ, M. (2005). *The Theory and Practice of Group Psychotherapy, 5th edition.* NY: Basic Books.

ZEBROWITZ, L.A., (1990), *Social Perception,* Pacific Grove, CA: Brooks/Cole Publishers.

ZUNKER, V.G., (1994), *Using Assessment Results for Career Development,* 4th Edition. Pacific Grove, CA: Brooks/Cole Publishers.

TEST I
Test I; Part I: Sample Selected Response Questions

Directions: Read each item and select the best response.

1. **The process of an active organism exhibiting controlled behavior is called:**
   (Rigorous) (Skill 1.1)

   A. Operant Conditioning

   B. Modeling

   C. Counterconditioning

   D. Transference

2. **The stages of life in Erik Erikson's psychosocial theory include all of the following except:**
   (Average Rigor) (Skill 1.1)

   A. Innocence vs. Generativity

   B. Basic Trust vs. Basic Mistrust

   C. Identity vs. Role Confusion

   D. Ego Integrity vs. Despair

3. **Which of the following are not schools of thought in psychoanalytic and psychodynamic theory:**
   (Rigorous) (Skill 1.1)

   A. Object relations and ego psychology

   B. Object relations and reinforcement

   C. Multimodal therapy and attachment theory

   D. Multimodal therapy and reinforcement

4. **Behavior theory is based on all of the following except:**
   (Average Rigor) (Skill 1.1)

   A. Developmental stages

   B. Conditioning

   C. Learning theory

   D. The ability to change

5. Around age 9 or 10, children experience all the following physical changes except:
   (Easy) (Skill 1.2)

   A. Hormonal shifts

   B. Growth spurts

   C. Additional teeth and a change in jaw size

   D. New body hair

6. Developmental milestones:
   (Average Rigor) (Skill 1.2)

   A. Clearly identify where a child falls in a specific area of growth

   B. Serve as guideposts

   C. Cannot be relied upon

   D. Are significantly different for boys and girls

7. Children's development is affected by all of the following factors except:
   (Average Rigor) (Skill 1.2)

   A. Gender and race

   B. Religion

   C. Their caregivers' emotional availability

   D. Nutrition

8. Factors related to homelessness or migrant worker status may make it difficult for students to:
   (Rigorous) (Skill 1.3)

   A. Get a job after high school

   B. Get to school and/or attend in class

   C. Succeed in school

   D. Make friends at school

9. Stressors that may affect a student's school performance include all of the following except:
   (Rigorous) (Skill 2.1)

   A. Mental health issues

   B. Having a single parent

   C. Losing a parent to death or divorce

   D. Being harassed at school

10. Possible signs of child abuse do not include:
    (Easy) (Skill 2.2)

    A. Old clothing

    B. Frequent bone fractures

    C. Self-destructive behavior

    D. Poor hygiene

11. Indications of substance abuse do not include:
    (Easy) (Skill 2.3)

    A. Attention problems

    B. Non-participation in athletic activities

    C. Bizarre behavior

    D. Unawareness of surroundings

12. All of the following are signs of anorexia nervosa except:
    (Average Rigor) (Skill 2.4)

    A. Malnutrition

    B. Behavior regression

    C. No outward signs

    D. Recognizable weight loss

13. When students self-injure, they:
    (Average Rigor) (Skill 2.4)

    A. Are suicidal

    B. Are overly focused on what others think of them

    C. Do it primarily to get attention

    D. Are expressing emotional pain in a physical way

14. Stages of human development as outlined by Jean Piaget include all of the following except:
    (Average Rigor) (Skill 3.1)

    A. Sensorimotor Stage

    B. Concrete Operational Stage

    C. Cultural and Environmental Stage

    D. Formal Operational Stage

15. Categories of theories of learning are all the following except:
    (Rigorous) (Skill 3.1)

    A. Behavioristic

    B. Functionalistic

    C. Associationistic

    D. Cognitive

16. The process of learning is not impacted by:
    (Average Rigor) (Skill 3.1)

    A. Past experiences

    B. Environmental factors

    C. Psychosexual stages

    D. Mental processes

17. **The success of a child in school does not depend on:** *(Rigorous) (Skill 3.2)*

    A. Class size

    B. Home attitude towards education

    C. Initial positive introduction to the school experience

    D. Addressing the specific needs of each child

18. **Individual learning styles can be expressed in relation to all the following except:** *(Rigorous) (Skill 3.2)*

    A. Environmental factors

    B. Emotional factors

    C. Intelligence quotients

    D. Sociological elements

19. **Positive school environments have all of the following characteristics except:** *(Easy) (Skill 4.1)*

    A. Strict rules

    B. Clear adult leadership

    C. Respect for diversity

    D. Policies and procedures to ensure the safety of everyone in the school community

20. **A positive school environment:** *(Average rigor) (Skill 4.1)*

    A. Is the primary responsibility of the school counselor

    B. Cannot be effectively determined without good testing instruments

    C. Is created by an attitude of collaboration and care

    D. Is difficult to achieve in today's world

21. **Effects of stereotyping and prejudice on victims do not include:** *(Rigorous) (Skill 4.2)*

    A. Confrontation of the perpetrator by the victim

    B. The development of a sense of inferiority

    C. The development of a persecution complex

    D. Thoughts of violence toward the perpetrator

22. **Violence prevention programs do not include:**
    (Rigorous) (Skill 4.3)

    A. Conflict resolution seminars

    B. Behavior modification programs

    C. Training faculty and staff to intervene before violent confrontations occur

    D. Instituting a boxing program to train students to protect themselves

23. **The occupational environments of Holland's theory do not include:**
    (Rigorous) (Skill 5.1)

    A. Artistic and social

    B. Realistic and conventional

    C. Enterprising and investigative

    D. Hostile and negative

24. **Super's theory of vocations is based upon all of the following except:**
    (Rigorous) (Skill 5.1)

    A. The inheritance of psychic energies

    B. The development of self-concepts

    C. External conditions that dictate the expression of self-concepts vocationally

    D. Developmental behavior theory

25. **Similarities in theories of vocational choice are all of the following except:**
    (Average Rigor) (Skill 5.1)

    A. They describe the relationship between two sets of observations

    B. They consider family influence on vocational choice a primary consideration

    C. They are usually based upon personality theory

    D. They emphasize the same types of critical periods in career development

26. **Decision making occurs at all the following critical points in career development except:**
    (Rigorous) (Skill 5.2)

    A. When a student enters high school

    B. In selecting an entry level job

    C. When selecting education plans

    D. In changing jobs

27. **In evaluating education and career materials all of the following should be considered except:**
    (Average Rigor) (Skill 6.1)

    A. Appropriate vocabulary for the targeted age and reading level

    B. Verified accuracy of the information

    C. Material from advertisements and trade organizations

    D. The avoidance of biased and stereotyping images

28. **In evaluating the content of career information, all of the following areas should be included except:**
    (Average Rigor) (Skill 6.1)

    A. The impressions of the reader as indicated by filling out an evaluation form

    B. The preparation required for entry level jobs

    C. The work setting and conditions of the career

    D. The long-term employment outlook

29. **Sources of information on education and vocational choices include:**
    (Average Rigor) (Skill 6.2)

    A. Neighbors and relatives

    B. American Trade School Directory

    C. The career guide of private schools *Getting Skilled, Getting Ahead*

    D. The local library

30. **Shadowing is not:**
    (Easy) (Skill 6.2)

    A. Spending an extended period of time with a particular person in a chosen field

    B. A paid experience

    C. A learning experience by the student and the business volunteer

    D. Experiencing the daily routine of a particular business

31. **The role of the counselor in assisting students in exploring career and educational options includes all the following except:**
    (Rigorous) (Skill 6.2)

    A. Have material for exploration easily accessible

    B. Support and encourage students in their search for career choices

    C. Help students form realistic decisions

    D. Explain career choice theories to them

32. **Post secondary education opportunities are not offered in:**
    (Average Rigor) (Skill 6.2)

    A. Vocational training

    B. Community colleges

    C. The military

    D. Practical experience

33. **Post-secondary educational opportunities do not depend on:**
    (Average Rigor) (Skill 6.2)

    A. The type of career in which the individual has an interest

    B. The abilities of the individual

    C. The social status of the individual

    D. The costs involved in attending

34. **Reliable sources of information on scholarships and financial aid do not include:**
    (Easy) (Skill 6.3)

    A. The guidance counselor

    B. Local scholarships

    C. Newspaper advertisements and paid financial aid sources

    D. Local and guidance department libraries

35. **Financial aid specifically earmarked for women and minorities is least likely to be found in:**
    (Average Rigor) (Skill 6.3)

    A. General financial aid references

    B. Minority and women's organizations

    C. The publication "The Higher Education Money Book for Women and Minorities"

    D. Local minority houses of worship

36. **The major steps in Zunker's model for using assessment results in developmental career counseling are all of the following except:**
    (Rigorous) (Skill 7.1)

    A. Analyzing needs

    B. Establishing the purpose of the test

    C. Administering a complete battery of tests

    D. Utilizing the results of assessment

37. **Effective study skills do not include:**
    (Easy) (Skill 7.2)

    A. Learning the material and then putting it aside until there is an exam scheduled

    B. Studying every day at a certain time

    C. Taking good notes

    D. Reviewing frequently

38. **In helping students to make decisions, steps in the process do not include:**
    (Average Rigor) (Skill 7.2)

    A. Defining the problem

    B. Listing all the options

    C. Surveying family, friends, and peers

    D. Formulating goals in relation to outcomes

39. **With regard to counseling, it is beyond the scope of the school counselor's role to:**
    (Average Rigor) (Skill 8.1)

    A. Provide individual and group counseling

    B. Provide crisis intervention

    C. Provide family consultation

    D. Provide mental health evaluations

40. The thinking through of irrational thoughts that have resulted in emotional problems is the basis of this theory
    (Rigorous) (Skill 8.2)

    A. Reality Therapy

    B. Gestalt Therapy

    C. Behavior Therapy

    D. Rational Emotive Behavior Therapy

41. Questions of freedom, choice and responsibility are addressed in:
    (Average Rigor) (Skill 8.2)

    A. Reality Therapy

    B. Existentialist Therapy

    C. Behavior Therapy

    D. Person-Centered Therapy

42. The therapist, in person-centered therapy, should have all the following personality characteristics except:
    (Average Rigor) (Skill 8.2)

    A. Genuineness

    B. Unconditional Positive Regard

    C. Empathic Understanding

    D. Polarized Thinking

43. The layers of neurosis in Perl's Gestalt theory of neurosis include all of the following except:
    (Rigorous) (Skill 8.2)

    A. Phobic Layer

    B. Impasse Layer

    C. Meaninglessness layer

    D. Explosive Layer

44. The WDEP model in reality theory includes all the following except:
    (Rigorous) (Skill 8.2)

    A. Wants

    B. Direction

    C. Evaluation

    D. Planning and Commitment

45. In applying counseling theories to specific situations, it is important that the counselor does all of the following except:
    (Average Rigor) (Skill 8.3)

    A. Create a rapport with the student

    B. Pick a theory to use and stick to that theory.

    C. Involve the student in the decision making process

    D. Encourage the student to make his/her own decisions.

46. **A concept not used in counseling theory is:**
    (Rigorous) (Skill 8.3)

    A. Changing behavior based on present situations

    B. Freud's division of development into five stages

    C. The correction of irrational and illogical thinking

    D. Learning ways to rationalize our behavior

47. **The keys to effective communication include all of the following except:**
    (Rigorous) (Skill 9.1)

    A. Being able to anticipate what the speaker is going to say

    B. Paying attention to nonverbal communication

    C. Asking for clarification

    D. Expressing oneself clearly and directly

48. **Elements of good listening skills include all the following except:**
    (Easy) (Skill 9.1)

    A. Involving strong emotions in the process of listening

    B. Being genuinely interested in the speaker

    C. Remembering what has been said

    D. Permitting a speaker to express him/herself fully

49. **Good responding skills include all of the following except:**
    (Easy) (Skill 9.1)

    A. Ability to show your feelings without inhibitions

    B. Reflecting back the other person's feelings

    C. Giving constructive feedback

    D. Maintaining eye contact

50. **Some current sources of professional information for counselors do not include:**
    (Easy) (Skill 9.2)

    A. Professional journals

    B. Workshops and conventions

    C. Visitations to other school programs

    D. Teenage magazines

51. Topics for discussion in the initial interview with a student to gain rapport do not include:
    (Rigorous) (Skill 9.3)

    A. Academic progress

    B. Activities in which the student is participating

    C. Difficulties in school adjustment for the entering student

    D. Matters of discipline referral

52. Ways not to be effective in communicating information to students are:
    (Easy) (Skill 9.3)

    A. Through individual interviews

    B. Through contacting friends and parents

    C. Through home room visitations

    D. Encouraging the student to assess his or her interests and needs

53. Components of an orientation program should include each of the following except:
    (Easy) (Skill 9.4)

    A. Advance notice by mail

    B. Invitations to the entire community

    C. A tour of the facilities

    D. Introduction of counselors and administrators to students and parents with a description of their roles

54. A disadvantage of group counseling is:
    (Average Rigor) (Skill 10.1)

    A. The presence of a built in support system

    B. A non-threatening atmosphere

    C. The ability to substitute the group for the real world, permitting the client unlimited time to make adjustments

    D. The counselor can reach more clients

55. **Limitations of group counseling are all of the following except:**
    (Average Rigor) (Skill 10.1)

    A. There is pressure to accept group values without analyzing them

    B. The counselor has to deal with a diverse population

    C. People sometimes function poorly in groups

    D. Individuals in the group can justify their present status by reinforcement from the group

56. **Group dynamics include all the following except:**
    (Rigorous) (Skill 10.2)

    A. A political ideology built on the concept of the organization and management of groups

    B. The employment of specific techniques and concepts to keep the group vitalized

    C. A branch of knowledge concerned with groups and their interactions, and interactions with other groups and individuals

    D. A description of individual behavior

57. **Group dynamics is all the following except:**
    (Rigorous) (Skill 10.2)

    A. An emphasis on empirical research and theory

    B. A branch of knowledge concerned mainly with the way groups form

    C. The relationships of groups with observable phenomena

    D. The interrelationship of all social science disciplines

58. **The need for specialized programs may be indicated by all of the following except:**
    (Rigorous) (Skill 11.1)

    A. Classroom management problems

    B. Targeted grant money

    C. A formal needs assessment

    D. Teacher or counselor observations

59. **All of the following are good prevention approaches except:**
(Average Rigor) (Skill 11.2)

   A. Informing parent/guardian(s) about their child's behavior in the school setting

   B. Programs on conflict resolution and communication skills

   C. Anger management groups

   D. Special programs such as the Lunch Bunch

60. **In using students as a resource in peer leadership the counselor should:**
(Average Rigor) (Skill 11.2)

   A. Not be present when students are conducting a group

   B. Choose the leaders from potential drop-outs

   C. Try not to let parents know what the process involves

   D. Have the student leaders go through an extensive period of training by a professional

Test I; Part II: Sample Constructed Response Assignments

Use the information described in each assignment to complete the tasks that follow.

INDIVIDUAL DEVELOPMENT AND LEARNING:
An eight-year-old girl has recently moved to the school district with her family and entered third grade.

- Describe some of the developmental and life issues this student may face.
- Address how these issues may affect her learning process.

Write your answer here:

COUNSELING AND GUIDANCE:
The school counselor is implementing a peer mediation program for all ninth graders.

- Describe key elements of the program curriculum.
- Address the strategies that will be used to teach this curriculum.

Write your answer here:

Test II; Part I: Sample Selected Response Questions

Directions: Read each item and select the best response.

1. Consultation process models include all the following except:
   (Easy) (Skill 12.1)

   A. Doctor/patient model

   B. Friend of the family model

   C. Behavior consultation model

   D. Mental health consultation model

2. The role of consultants in problem solving processes does not include functioning:
   (Average Rigor) (Skill 12.1)

   A. As an advocate

   B. As an expert in a particular area

   C. As a school official

   D. As a process specialist

3. Procedures in the consultation process include all except:
   (Average Rigor) (Skill 12.1)

   A. Relationship building

   B. Monitoring of the process of behavior change by a neutral party

   C. Evaluation and summarization

   D. Diagnosis of the problem

4. The consultation process in the school setting does not include:
   (Rigorous) (Skill 12.1)

   A. Eliminating the need to counsel students

   B. The meeting of a consultant and a consultee

   C. The solving of a specific problem

   D. Involving consultees (people seeking solutions to student problems)

5. **The role the counselor can take in assisting participants in the consultation process does not include:**
   (Average Rigor) (Skill 12.2)

   A. Demonstrating classroom behavior management techniques

   B. Describing the nature of the problem

   C. Teaching specific skills

   D. Helping devise strategies to change behaviors

6. **In the consultation process, communicating student's needs to others does not include:**
   (Average Rigor) (Skill 12.2)

   A. Making a judgment by the counselor to others as to what is best for the student

   B. Clarifying the needs of the student with the student

   C. Opening lines of communication between the consultee and the student by having open dialogue

   D. Balancing the needs of the student and the consultee so each can understand the other's position

7. **Procedures for successful communication with parent/guardian(s) in the consultation process do not include:**
   (Average Rigor) (Skill 12.2)

   A. Informing parents frequently as to the progress of the resolution of the problem

   B. Using parents as a valuable source of information about the student

   C. Accepting parents ideas for behavior modification

   D. Explaining the problem in simple language as parents are probably unaware of all ramifications

8. **Contributions of parents to the consultation process do not include:**
   (Easy) (Skill 12.2)

   A. Family and medical history

   B. Usually parents do not contribute to the process, as they are uncooperative

   C. Monitoring the child at home

   D. A positive attitude

9. **In gathering data for the implementation of a consultation, the counselor should not:**
   (Average Rigor) (Skill 12.2)

   A. Examine the permanent record card for test scores and patterns

   B. Gather medical and discipline history

   C. Consult with an administrator about the student's family history

   D. Talk with the student's teachers to see if they are experiencing the same type of problems

10. **In conducting a consultation follow-up, the counselor should not:**
    (Rigorous) (Skill 12.2)

    A. Gradually decrease participation in the process

    B. Reevaluate after a period of time

    C. Interview the consultee to determine if there is continuing progress

    D. Interview the student and parents in regards to their satisfaction with the consultation

11. **In evaluating the results of consultation, all the following factors should be considered except:**
    (Rigorous) (Skill 12.2)

    A. The feelings of the student's parents as to the success of the process

    B. The report of the consultee as to the problem solving results

    C. An attitude change in the student

    D. Empirical results of an evaluation tool

12. **Family dynamics:**
    (Easy) (Skill 13.1)

    A. Are not relevant to the work of school counselor

    B. Can impact a student's behavior in school

    C. Always play a major role in a student's behavior problems

    D. Rarely affect a student in the school setting

13. **Elements of family dynamics include all of the following except:**
    (Rigorous) (Skill 13.1)

    A. Rules and roles within the family

    B. The reinforcement of individual behavior patterns via family interactions

    C. An "identified patient" who serves to divert the family from underlying problems

    D. The parent's childhood background

14. **Components of a program of parental contact do not include:**
    (Average Rigor) (Skill 13.2)

    A. Informing parents of information heard around the school regarding their child

    B. Creating a parent advisory committee

    C. Telephone contact with parents when students are doing well

    D. Small teas and home meetings to inform parents of procedures for their children to maximize education opportunities

15. **In interactions with school counselors and other school officials, parents and guardians need respect, information and:**
    (Average Rigor) (Skill 13.2)

    A. Positive feedback

    B. Confirmation that they are doing a good job with their child

    C. Validation and support

    D. Detailed descriptions of their child's interactions with peers and teachers

16. **In working with parents, a good model to utilize is:**
    (Easy) (Skill 13.2)

    A. Collaborative consultation

    B. Mental health consultation

    C. Family counseling

    D. Advising

17. The consultation process with parents does not include: (Rigorous) (Skill 13.2)

    A. Allowing them to vent their frustrations about the school and school officials

    B. Getting to the issue at hand as soon as possible

    C. Clearly delineating the next steps the parent needs to take

    D. Taking care not to make too many suggestions and overwhelm the parent

18. Data included in the initial referral of a child to a counselor should not include: (Average Rigor) (Skill 13.3)

    A. Unverified illegal behavior

    B. Academic history

    C. Behavior and discipline history

    D. Family history

19. Procedures for referring a student to an outside agency do not include: (Easy) (Skill 13.3)

    A. The counselor has evaluated a need for long-term counseling

    B. The parent feels the child has an emotional problem and asks for an evaluation

    C. The counselor is mandated to report a sexual abuse case

    D. The student doesn't like the counselor

20. School counselors may provide information about which of the following resources for families: (Easy) (Skill 13.3)

    A. Mental health referrals

    B. Food banks and government aid programs

    C. Local support groups

    D. All of the above

21. **All but which of the following are important aspects of crisis intervention:** *(Easy) (Skill 14.1)*

    A. Accurate information for those affected by the situation

    B. The latest news reports about the crisis

    C. A school crisis response plan

    D. A systematic way to inform school personnel about the actions to be taken

22. **Crisis responders need all of the following except:** *(Easy) (Skill 14.1)*

    A. A chance to debrief and get support from colleagues

    B. Clarity about roles and responsibilities

    C. Mandatory post-trauma counseling

    D. Adequate training and follow-up

23. **An effective advocate does not:** *(Average Rigor) (Skill 15.1)*

    A. Share all information gathered about a particular situation.

    B. Speak up for those who may not have a voice or been heard in the past.

    C. Try to facilitate change

    D. Watch for trends that may indicate underserved populations

24. **Which of the following is not a form of assessment administered by school counselors:** *(Easy) (Skill 16.1)*

    A. Achievement tests

    B. Intelligence tests

    C. College entrance exams

    D. Performance tests

25. **A condition that does not affect testing results is:** *(Rigorous) (Skill 16.1)*

   A. The physical and mental condition of the testee

   B. The testing room environment

   C. The colors of the clothes the proctors are wearing

   D. The validity of the test

26. **All the following are advantages of testing except:** *(Average Rigor) (Skill 16.1)*

   A. As a way to get multiple test interpretations

   B. As a way to help students recognize and use the resources they have

   C. As a way to present meaningful information to the student for decision making

   D. As a way to help identify options for the future

27. **Disadvantages of testing are all the following except:** *(Rigorous) (Skill 16.1)*

   A. The possibility of results being used improperly

   B. The possibility of the student misinterpreting the test results

   C. The inherent subjectivity of tests administered for counseling purposes

   D. Using the test to predict future behavior

28. **Informal forms of assessment include all of the following except:** *(Average Rigor) (Skill 16.1)*

   A. Behavioral observation

   B. Learning styles inventories

   C. Sentence completion

   D. Interviewing peers

29. In the administration of tests, procedures should include all the following except:
    (Rigorous) (Skill 16.2)

    A. Safeguarding the tests

    B. Informing the students of the nature of the test by giving them questions from the test

    C. Guarding the tests in the exam room when students have access to the room

    D. Guarding the tests by not leaving them where students and non- authorized personnel have access

30. The inaccuracy of test results caused by chance is called:
    (Rigorous) (Skill 17.1)

    A. Standardization

    B. Standard Error of Measurement

    C. Standard Score

    D. Derived Score

31. A statistical concept that measures the relationship between two factors in test validity is:
    (Rigorous) (Skill 17.1)

    A. Reliability Coefficient

    B. Standard Deviation

    C. Raw Score

    D. Correlation Coefficient

32. The specific interval between bands of scores, with each interval indicating a different level of achievement, is called:
    (Average Rigor) (Skill 17.1)

    A. Reliability Coefficient

    B. Standard Deviation

    C. Raw Score

    D. Correlation Coefficient

33. **If tests need to be interpreted in a group the counselor should not:**
    (Average Rigor) (Skill 18.1)

    A. Announce individual test scores

    B. Explain the norm group to which the students have been compared

    C. Provide for private individual interpretation for students

    D. Explain statistics of the test so students can understand the meaning of their scores

34. **The written report of test results and interpretation should not:**
    (Average Rigor) (Skill 18.1)

    A. Be written in understandable language

    B. Always include charts and graphs

    C. Be disseminated on a need to know basis

    D. Be written in the language of testing

35. **In accurately reporting test results for interpretation by others all the following guidelines should be used except:**
    (Rigorous) (Skill 18.1)

    A. A uniform method of recording should be employed

    B. Consistency in language used should be employed

    C. The purpose, limitations, and the validity of the test should be stated

    D. The receiver of the results should be required to contact the counselor in order to receive the counselor's candid opinion

36. **In interpreting test results the counselor should not:**
    (Average Rigor) (Skill 18.2)

    A. Relate the results to the goals that had previously been determined

    B. Provide for individual interpretation

    C. Wait to interpret the tests when the student is scheduling the following year's courses

    D. Give the student input into the interpretation of the test results

37. **In interpreting test results to other professionals and parents, the counselor does not always have to:**
    (Average Rigor) (Skill 18.2)

    E. Be thoroughly familiar with the test

    F. Let other staff members see the results of the test

    G. Notify the student that the counselor will be sharing the results with their parent/guardian(s)

    H. Work with the parents in a counseling relationship to help them understand their child's abilities

38. **In interpreting testing data from other professionals and testing firms, the counselor should do all the following except:**
    (Average Rigor) (Skill 18.2)

    A. Understand the material in the report

    B. Go right to the summary and not worry about the technical aspects of the report

    C. Contact the writer of the report for clarification if needed

    D. Refer to the testing manual for clarification if needed

39. **A good guidance program does not include:**
    (Easy) (Skill 19.1)

    A. A pay scale for counselors higher than other staff members in order to attract quality people

    B. An adequate budget to supply the basic tools needed for the program

    C. Trained, certified, professional counselors

    D. A mission statement

40. **The goals of the guidance program should not include:**
    (Rigorous) (Skill 19.1)

    A. Acquisition of academic skills by the student population commensurate with their abilities

    B. Acquisition of personal insights by students

    C Learned ability to make intelligent choices

    D. Selection of a lifetime career

41. Techniques to let the community know what is happening in guidance do not include:
    (Easy) (Skill 19.1)

    A. A guidance newsletter

    B. A letter to the editor regarding the school board cutting guidance staff

    C. Speaking about the guidance program to local civic organizations

    D. Involving community leaders as members of an advisory board

42. The type of research in which counselors would engage is not:
    (Rigorous) (Skill 19.2)

    A. Historical

    B. Single subject experimental

    C. Assessment and evaluation

    D. Qualitative

43. The purpose of research in which a working counselor would not engage is:
    (Average Rigor) (Skill 19.2)

    A. Basic research to obtain knowledge without the need for practical application

    B. Applied research to obtain general ways to improve education

    C. To develop a theory for creating generalizations

    D. Action research to immediately apply results to a specific problem

44. The research evaluation stages of the CIPP model do not include:
    (Rigorous) (Skill 19.2)

    A. Context evaluation

    B. Process evaluation

    C. Input evaluation

    D. Program evaluation

45. **Formative evaluation does not involve:**
    (Rigorous) (Skill 19.3)

    A. Collection of data in the developmental stage of research

    B. Collection of data in the implementation stage of research

    C. Collection of data after a program has been in place a period of time

    A. Collection of data when the research is in the operational stage

46. **In conducting a program needs assessment the following individuals should be included:**
    (Rigorous) (Skill 19.3)

    A. Students only

    B. Administrators only

    C. People in the community who have no students in school

    D. The community, students, staff, administrators, and parents

47. **The determining factors of the worth of a program do not include:**
    (Rigorous) (Skill 19.4)

    A. How well the program fits preconceived ideas of intended outcomes

    B. Statistical significance

    C. Interpretation of the meaning of the results

    D. The practicality of implementing the program into every day use

48. **Program objectives are:**
    (Rigorous) (Skill 19.4)

    A. Created to fit the outcomes of the research

    B. Readjusted as the need arises

    C. Determined after the program has been operational for a period of time

    D. Formulated before the research is instituted

49. **In evaluating a newly created program, the counselor should:**
    (Rigorous) (Skill 19.4)

    A. Ask the guidance staff if they think the program is working

    B. Ask students informally what they think of the program

    C. Conduct an extensive evaluation of everyone involved that includes surveys, questionnaires, and observations

    D. After three months, evaluate the program and make a recommendation

50. **Before introducing new and innovative programs to the guidance curriculum the counselor should first:**
    (Rigorous) (Skill 19.4)

    A. Ask the administration for a budget for the program

    B. Conduct a needs assessment survey

    C. Arrange for a pilot program

    D. Contact Board of Education members to get them to agree on the implementation of the program

51. **Guidelines for ethical behavior written in the ACA Code of Ethics and Standards of Practice include all of the following areas except:**
    (Rigorous) (Skill 20.1)

    A. Penalties for specific ethical violations

    B. Confidentiality

    C. Resolving of ethical issues

    D. Relationships with other professionals

52. **The purpose of the National Board of Certified Counselors (NBCC) is to:**
    (Average Rigor) (Skill 20.1)

    A. Issue practice credentials

    B. Resolve ethical issues

    C. Certify professionals to assure a high level of competence

    D. Bargain for higher salaries for guidance professionals

53. When an ethical issue arises in a counselor's practice the counselor should:
    (Average Rigor) (Skill 20.1)

    A. Refer to the ACA code of Ethics

    B. Decide what to do immediately so the problem will not linger

    C. Ask the client what to do

    D. Consult with the Board of Education

54. Continuing professional development is important for school counselors for all of the following reasons except:
    (Easy) (Skill 20.2)

    A. To keep abreast of changes in professional practices and standards

    B. To utilize all available monies in the budget for staff development

    C. To be refreshed and renewed as a professional

    D. To further develop counseling skills

55. Parents, guardians, and students have a right to all the following records except:
    (Rigorous) (Skill 21.1)

    A. Copies of all records relating to the student

    B. Copies of all student records containing comparisons of the student with other students

    C. All the student's records maintained by public institutions

    D. A list of all types of records directly related to the student

56. The rights of parents, students, and guardians do not include:
    (Average Rigor) (Skill 21.1)

    A. Right of access

    B. Right of privacy

    C. Right to challenge and a hearing

    D. Right to alter the written record if they feel it is not true

57. Who are not the people limited to a "need to know" basis with regard to student assessment data:
 (Average Rigor) (Skill 21.1)

 A. The newspapers

 B. School personnel

 C. The counselor, school psychologist, school social worker and principal

 D. Attorneys

58. Written permission must be obtained to release assessment data from:
 (Average Rigor) (Skill 21.1)

 A. The counselor

 B. The student over 18 or the student's parent or guardian

 C. The Board of Education

 D. The teacher who generated the assessment data

59. The intent of the Individuals with Disabilities Act of 1975 was all of the following except:
 (Rigorous) (Skill 21.2)

 A. To give children with disabilities special services to make up for past discriminations

 B. To give children with disabilities a free and appropriate education

 C. To provide for the needs of children with disabilities

 D. To prevent discrimination against children with disabilities

60. School counselors are required to report suspected child abuse and neglect by all of the following people except:
 (Rigorous) (Skill 21.3)

 A. A parent or guardian

 B. Someone living in the child's home

 C. The child's caregiver

 D. A grandparent

Test II; Part II: Sample Constructed Response Assignments

Use the information described in each assignment to complete the tasks that follow.

CONSULTATION AND COLLABORATION:
A well-loved custodian at the middle school died suddenly over the weekend. The school principal has asked the school counselor to help the students and families cope with this loss.

- Describe what strategies the counselor might employ.
- Discuss the value of these strategies.

Write your answer here:

PROFESSIONAL IDENTITY AND PRACTICE:

The grandparent of a high school senior contacts the school counselor about the senior's recent performance test results and offers information about the student.

- Describe the circumstances under which the counselor may or may not discuss the test results with the grandparent.
- Discuss what other steps the counselor needs to take regarding disclosure and notification as a result of contact with the grandparent.

Write your answer here:

TEACHER CERTIFICATION STUDY GUIDE

ANSWER KEY: Selected Response Questions

Test I

1. A	17. A	33. C	49. A
2. A	18. C	34. C	50. D
3. D	19. A	35. A	51. D
4. A	20. C	36. C	52. B
5. C	21. A	37. A	53. B
6. B	22. D	38. C	54. C
7. B	23. D	39. D	55. B
8. B	24. A	40. D	56. D
9. B	25. B	41. B	57. B
10. B	26. A	42. D	58. B
11. B	27. C	43. C	59. A
12. C	28. A	44. B	60. D
13. D	29. A	45. B	
14. C	30. B	46. D	
15. A	31. D	47. A	
16. C	32. D	48. A	

Test II

1. B	17. C	33. A	49. C
2. C	18. A	34. B	50. B
3. B	19. D	35. D	51. A
4. A	20. D	36. C	52. C
5. A	21. B	37. B	53. A
6. A	22. C	38. B	54. B
7. D	23. A	39. A	55. B
8. B	24. B	40. D	56. D
9. C	25. C	41. B	57. C
10. A	26. A	42. B	58. B
11. D	27. D	43. C	59. A
12. B	28. D	44. D	60. D
13. D	29. B	45. C	
14. A	30. B	46. D	
15. C	31. D	47. A	
16. A	32. B	48. D	

Rigor Table

	EASY 20%	AVERAGE RIGOR 40%	RIGOROUS 40%
TEST I	5, 10, 11, 19, 30, 34, 37, 48, 49, 50, 52, 53	2, 4, 6, 7, 12, 13, 14, 20, 25, 27, 28, 29, 32, 33, 35, 38, 39, 41, 42, 45, 54, 55, 59, 60	1, 3, 8, 9, 15, 16, 17, 18, 21, 22, 23, 24, 26, 31, 36, 40, 43, 44, 46, 47, 51, 56, 57, 58
TEST II	1, 8, 12, 16, 19, 20, 21, 22, 24, 39, 41, 54	2, 3, 5, 6, 7, 9, 14, 15, 18, 23, 26, 28, 32, 33, 34, 36, 37, 38, 43, 52, 53, 56, 57, 58	4, 10, 11, 13, 17, 25, 27, 29, 30, 31, 35, 40, 42, 44, 45, 46, 47, 48, 49, 50, 51, 55, 59, 60

TEST I
Test I; Part I: Sample Selected Response Answers and Rationales

Directions: Read each item and select the best response.

1. The process of an active organism exhibiting controlled behavior is called:
   (Rigorous) (Skill 1.1)

   A. Operant Conditioning

   B. Modeling

   C. Counterconditioning

   D. Transference

Answer: A. Operant Conditioning

Counter-conditioning is the process of redoing the behaviors that have caused the problem and performing new behaviors that can eliminate the problem. Transference is a process where the client projects feelings concerning past interactions onto the therapist within the counseling relationship. Modeling involves observing behavior of those we wish to imitate and then performing the behaviors we have observed.

2. The stages of life in Erik Erikson's psychosocial theory include all of the following except:
   (Average Rigor) (Skill 1.1)

   A. Innocence vs. Generativity

   B. Basic Trust vs. Basic Mistrust

   C. Identity vs. Role Confusion

   D. Ego Integrity vs. Despair

Answer: A. Innocence vs. Generativity

Innocence is not one of Erikson's stages. Generativity vs. Stagnation is the stage when maturity is achieved. The task here is to establish and guide the next generation and come to terms with one's dreams and accomplishments.

3. Which of the following are not schools of thought in psychoanalytic and psychodynamic theory:
   (Rigorous) (Skill 1.1)

   A. Object relations and ego psychology

   B. Object relations and reinforcement

   C. Multimodal therapy and attachment theory

   D. Multimodal therapy and reinforcement

Answer: D. Multimodal therapy and reinforcement

Multimodal therapy is a form of cognitive behavioral therapy. Reinforcement is a concept in behaviorism that says a specific response to a behavior that increases the probability of that behavior being repeated.

4. Behavior theory is based on all of the following except:
   (Average Rigor) (Skill 1.1)

   A. Developmental stages

   B. Conditioning

   C. Learning theory

   D. The ability to change

Answer: A. Developmental stages

Developmental stages are not considered in behaviorism.

TEACHER CERTIFICATION STUDY GUIDE

5. Around age 9 or 10, children experience all the following physical changes except:
   (Easy) (Skill 1.2)

   A. Hormonal shifts

   B. Growth spurts

   C. Additional teeth and a change in jaw size

   D. New body hair

Answer: C. Additional teeth and a change in jaw size

At preadolescence (beginning around age 9 years and lasting till puberty), children experience hormonal shifts, growth spurts and new body hair. However, they do not experience a change in their jaw size.

6. Developmental milestones:
   (Average Rigor) (Skill 1.2)

   A. Clearly identify where a child falls in a specific area of growth

   B. Serve as guideposts

   C. Cannot be relied upon

   D. Are significantly different for boys and girls

Answer: B. Serve as guideposts

Developmental milestones are guideposts against which children's growth and developmental can be measured. They are not set in stone but do provide generally reliable markers. Although there are some gender differences, especially at preadolescence, overall boys and girls follow similar developmental pathways.

7. **Children's development is affected by all of the following factors except:**
   (Average Rigor) (Skill 1.2)

   A. Gender and race

   B. Religion

   C. Their caregivers' emotional availability

   D. Nutrition

Answer: B. Religion

Development is affected by many different factors, one of which is NOT religion.

8. **Factors related to homelessness or migrant worker status may make it difficult for students to:**
   (Rigorous) (Skill 1.3)

   A. Get a job after high school

   B. Get to school and/or attend in class

   C. Succeed in school

   D. Make friends at school

Answer: B. Get to school and/or attend in class

Post-traumatic stress, poverty and other life concerns may interfere with a student's attendance. She or he may not come to school or may have difficulty paying attention in class. However, students from all families can succeed in school, make friends, and get a job after high school with the right support and motivation.

9. **Stressors that may affect a student's school performance include all of the following except:**
   (Rigorous) (Skill 2.1)

   A. Mental health issues

   B. Having a single parent

   C. Losing a parent to death or divorce

   D. Being harassed at school

Answer: B. Having a single parent

Being the child of a single parent is not a stressor in and of itself. Losing a parent to death or divorce, coping with mental health or addiction issues at home, experiencing difficulties at school with peers, child abuse and others issues generally are stressors for children that affect school performance.

10. **Possible signs of child abuse do not include:**
    (Easy) (Skill 2.2)

    A. Frequent bone fractures

    B. Old clothing

    C. Self-destructive behavior

    D. Poor hygiene

Answer: B. Old clothing

It would be making assumption about the state of the clothing and the family situation. If there is a concern about a student's welfare, the counselor can follow up using appropriate channels and methods.

11. **Indications of substance abuse do not include:**
    (Easy) (Skill 2.3)

    A. Attention problems

    B. Non-participation in athletic activities

    C. Bizarre behavior

    D. Unawareness of surroundings

Answer: B. Non-participation in athletic activities

Students with substance abuse issues may elect or continue to participate in athletic opportunities. However, if there is a pattern of inconsistent attendance or exhibits of behavior that is not customary for the student (providing that there is not a known medical or physical condition), follow-up is indicated.

12. **All of the following are signs of anorexia nervosa except:**
    (Average Rigor) (Skill 2.4)

    A. Malnutrition

    B. Behavior regression

    C. No outward signs

    D. Recognizable weight loss

Answer: C. No outward signs

This answer is self-explanatory. There are significant outward signs when a person is struggling with anorexia.

13. **When students self-injure, they:**
    (Average Rigor) (Skill 2.4)

    A. Are suicidal

    B. Are overly focused on what others think of them

    C. Do it primarily to get attention

    D. Are expressing emotional pain in a physical way

Answer: D. Are expressing emotional pain in a physical way

Self-injury is an attempt to convey and release emotional pain and tension through cutting, hitting or other form of self-harm. While students who self-injure may need attention or help, they generally don't self-injure just to get attention nor are they suicidal. They may or may not be concerned with what others think of them.

14. **Stages of human development as outlined by Jean Piaget include all of the following except:**
    (Average Rigor) (Skill 3.1)

    A. Sensorimotor Stage

    B. Concrete Operational Stage

    C. Cultural and Environmental Stage

    D. Formal Operational Stage

Answer: C. Cultural and Environment Stage

While cultural and environmental factors may play a role throughout one's development, it is not a stage as defined by Piaget.

15. **Categories of theories of learning are all the following except:**
    (Rigorous) (Skill 3.1)

    A. Behavioristic

    B. Functionalistic

    C. Associationistic

    D. Cognitive

Answer: A. Behavioristic

Theories of counseling, personality and learning are interrelated and address behavior. The three categories of learning theories are functionalistic, associationistic and cognitive.

16. **The process of learning is not impacted by:**
    (Rigorous) (Skill 3.1)

    A. Past experiences

    B. Environmental factors

    C. Psychosexual stages

    D. Mental processes

Answer: C. Psychosexual stages

Psychosexual stages are a concept in psychoanalytic theory and are not included in discussions of learning theories.

17. **The success of a child in school does not depend on:**
    (Rigorous) (Skill 3.2)

    A. Class size

    B. Home attitude towards education

    C. Initial positive introduction to the school experience

    D. Addressing the specific needs of each child

Answer: A. Class size

County or district guidelines may make stipulations on how many students may be in a classroom. However, the success of a student can involve many but class size is not one of these factors. This is a common educational misconception.

18. **Individual learning styles can be expressed in relation to all the following except:**
    (Rigorous) (Skill 3.2)

    A. Environmental factors

    B. Emotional factors

    C. Intelligence quotients

    D. Sociological elements

Answer: C. Intelligence quotients

Individual learning styles include environmental, emotional, sociological and physical elements. Learning styles do not measure and are not based on intelligence.

19. **Positive school environments have all of the following characteristics except:**
    (Easy) (Skill 4.1)

    A. Strict rules

    B. Clear adult leadership

    C. Respect for diversity

    D. Policies and procedures to ensure the safety of everyone in the school community

Answer: A. Strict rules

While clear policies and strong leadership are essential, strict rules generally do not contribute to creating positive school environments. At times, they may even have a detrimental effect, depending on the nature of the rules.

20. **A positive school environment:**
    (Average rigor) (Skill 4.1)

    A. Is the primary responsibility of the school counselor

    B. Cannot be effectively determined without good testing instruments

    C. Is created by an attitude of collaboration and care

    D. Is difficult to achieve in today's world

Answer: C. Is created by an attitude of collaboration and care

A caring approach and an actively collaborative style are major contributors to positive school environments. While schools counselors must be a part of this process, it is not their primary responsibility, nor can they effect such change alone.

21. **Effects of stereotyping and prejudice on victims do not include:**
    (Rigorous) (Skill 4.2)

    A. Confrontation of the perpetrator by the victim

    B. The development of a sense of inferiority

    C. The development of a persecution complex

    D. Thoughts of violence toward the perpetrator

Answer: A. Confrontation of the perpetrator by the victim

To confront a perpetrator could lead to a potentially dangerous altercation between to the victim and the perpetrator, although in some structured situations and with sufficient planning this can be a healing event for victim and/or perpetrator. However, such an interaction is not an *effect* of stereotyping and prejudice.

22. **Violence prevention programs do not include:**
    (Rigorous) (Skill 4.3)

    A. Conflict resolution seminars

    B. Behavior modification programs

    C. Training faculty and staff to intervene before violent confrontations occur

    D. Instituting a boxing program to train students to protect themselves

Answer: D. Instituting a boxing program to train students to protect themselves

Students can be taught to respect the rights of others by programs of cooperation and conflict resolution. The violence prevention program should not promote, encourage, or prepare students to engage in physical retaliation. A boxing program is outside the scope of violence prevention.

23. **The occupational environments of Holland's theory do not include:**
    (Rigorous) (Skill 5.1)

    A. Artistic and social

    B. Realistic and conventional

    C. Enterprising and investigative

    D. Hostile and negative

Answer: D. Hostile and negative

While some occupational settings may in fact be hostile and negative, these adjectives do not describe the occupational environments as defined by Holland.

24. **Super's theory of vocations is based upon all of the following except:**
    (Rigorous) (Skill 5.1)

    A. The inheritance of psychic energies

    B. The development of self-concepts

    C. External conditions that dictate the expression of self-concepts vocationally

    D. Developmental behavior theory

Answer: A. The inheritance of psychic energies

Psychic energy is defined as the drive that propels a person's behavior and psychological functioning. This is not part of Super's theory.

25. **Similarities in theories of vocational choice are all of the following except:**
    (Average Rigor) (Skill 5.1)

    A. They describe the relationship between two sets of observations

    B. They consider family influence on vocational choice a primary consideration

    C. They are usually based upon personality theory

    D. They emphasize the same types of critical periods in career development

Answer: B. They consider family influence on vocational choice a primary consideration

The primary influences on vocational choice include personality and level of education. Vocational choice theories place very little emphasis on the influence of family as a major factor. Family influence can have a direct impact on educational achievement but only an indirect, minor impact on vocational choice.

26. **Decision making occurs at all the following critical points in career development except:**
    (Rigorous) (Skill 5.2)

    A. When a student enters high school

    B. In selecting an entry level job

    C. When selecting education plans

    D. In changing jobs

Answer: A. When a student enters high school

According to Roe and Ginzberg, Ginzberg, Axelrad & Herm, the high school years mark a period of exploration in a person's career development. This process of exploration can provide insight to a possible career choice.

27. **In evaluating education and career materials all of the following should be considered except:**
    (Average Rigor) (Skill 6.1)

    A. Appropriate vocabulary for the targeted age and reading level

    B. Verified accuracy of the information

    C. Material from advertisements and trade organizations

    D. The avoidance of biased and stereotyping images

Answer: C. Material from advertisements and trade organizations

Counselors must use their research and investigative skills to discern appropriate education and career materials.

28. **In evaluating the content of career information, all of the following areas should be included except:**
    (Average Rigor) (Skill 6.1)

    A. The impressions of the reader as indicated by filling out an evaluation form

    B. The preparation required for entry-level jobs

    C. The work setting and conditions of the career

    D. The long-term employment outlook

Answer: A. The impressions of the reader as indicated by filling out an evaluation form

The phrase "impressions of the reader" denotes one of subjectivity instead of specific points that can provide the most comprehensive picture of a respective career. Guidelines for the preparation and evaluation of career and occupational literature have been compiled by the National Career Development Association (NCDA).

29. **Sources of information on education and vocational choices include:**
    (Average Rigor) (Skill 6.2)

    A. Neighbors and relatives

    B. American Trade School Directory

    C. The career guide of private schools *Getting Skilled, Getting Ahead*

    D. The local library

Answer: A. Neighbors and relatives

While neighbors and relatives can provide information about their experiences with careers or jobs they have held, the information gathered would be subjective and may not be relevant or accurate.

30. **Shadowing is not:**
    (Easy) (Skill 6.2)

    A. Spending an extended period of time with a particular person in a chosen field

    B. A paid experience

    C. A learning experience by the student and the business volunteer

    D. Experiencing the daily routine of a particular business

Answer: B. A paid experience

A paid experience or internship is provided with the understanding that services are being provided on behalf on an employee. The true shadowing experience should be experiential and have nothing to do with payment.

31. **The role of the counselor in assisting students in exploring career and educational options includes all the following except:**
    (Rigorous) (Skill 6.2)

    A. Have material for exploration easily accessible

    B. Support and encourage students in their search for career choices

    C. Help students form realistic decisions

    D. Explain career choice theories to them

Answer: D. Explain career choice theories to them

The counselor can use one or more career theories or orientations in order to provide a framework for the work they do with students. However, merely explaining theories to students is neither an effective use of the counselor's time nor does it provide practical applications by which the students can use to explore careers and related information.

32. **Post secondary education opportunities are not offered in:**
    (Average Rigor) (Skill 6.2)

    A. Vocational training

    B. Community colleges

    C. The military

    D. Practical experience

Answer: D. Practical experience

Post-secondary education lends itself to organized learning experiences, which at the end of a certain time interval, a degree is awarded to signify the completion or mastery of certain skills. While much can be learned from a practical experience such as internships or shadowing, an individual does not earn a degree or certificate. Options A, B, and C are opportunities that afford an individual to learn a skill set, be awarded a degree, and then apply for professional work experiences.

33. **Post-secondary educational opportunities do not depend on:**
    (Average Rigor) (Skill 6.2)

    A. The type of career in which the individual has an interest

    B. The abilities of the individual

    C. The social status of the individual

    D. The costs involved in attending

Answer: C. The social status of the individual.

Social status will only be a determining factor if an individual allows it to be.

34. **Reliable sources of information on scholarships and financial aid do not include:**
    (Easy) (Skill 6.3)

    A. The guidance counselor

    B. Local scholarships

    C. Newspaper advertisements and paid financial aid sources

    D. Local and guidance department libraries

Answer: C. Newspaper advertisements and paid financial aid sources

Counselors, parents and students need to be cautious about advertisements for scholarships and financial aid. It is important that such opportunities be thoroughly investigated. If money is being asked for up front in order to apply for a scholarship, applicants should not apply. It is likely that such an opportunity is a moneymaking scam. There are a variety of sources that can be used to determine if a source is legitimate.

35. Financial aid specifically earmarked for women and minorities is least likely to be found in:
    (Average Rigor) (Skill 6.3)

    A. General financial aid references

    B. Minority and women's organizations

    C. The publication "The Higher Education Money Book for Women and Minorities"

    D. Local minority houses of worship

Answer: A. General financial aid references

Options B, C, and D address the sources that are specific students seeking scholarships for minorities and women. It is important when seeking scholarships with specific criteria to research sources that provide that information.

36. The major steps in Zunker's model for using assessment results in developmental career counseling are all of the following except:
    (Rigorous) (Skill 7.1)

    A. Analyzing needs

    B. Establishing the purpose of the test

    C. Administering a complete battery of tests

    D. Utilizing the results of assessment

Answer: C. Administering a complete battery of tests

Zunker, with influence from other theorists, established a model for the use of assessment results in developmental career counseling. There are four major steps: analyzing needs, establishing the purpose of testing, determining the instruments to be used, and utilizing the results in decision making for training and education. Identifying specific tests are more useful than using a whole battery of tests.

37. **Effective study skills do not include:**
    (Easy) (Skill 7.2)

    A. Learning the material and then putting it aside until there is an exam scheduled

    B. Studying every day at a certain time

    C. Taking good notes

    D. Reviewing frequently

Answer: A. Learning the material and then putting it aside until there is an exam scheduled

The student will not retain the information if there is a large gap between the learning and the testing of the material.

38. **In helping students to make decisions, steps in the process do not include:**
    (Average Rigor) (Skill 7.2)

    A. Defining the problem

    B. Listing all the options

    C. Surveying family, friends, and peers

    D. Formulating goals in relation to outcomes

Answer: C. Surveying family, friends, and peers

Surveying denotes a process of information gathering from friends and family; it is not a step in the decision making process.

39. **With regard to counseling, it is beyond the scope of the school counselor's role to:**
    (Average Rigor) (Skill 8.1)

    A. Provide individual and group counseling

    B. Provide crisis intervention

    C. Provide family consultation

    D. Provide mental health evaluations

Answer: D. Provide mental health evaluations

Although school counselors may identify the need for a mental health evaluation, it is beyond the scope of their role and often their knowledge base to actually perform mental health evaluations. Referral to a community agency or private practitioner is most appropriate to meet students' evaluation needs.

40. **The thinking through of irrational thoughts that have resulted in emotional problems is the basis of this theory:**
    (Rigorous) (Skill 8.2)

    A. Reality Therapy

    B. Gestalt Therapy

    C. Behavior Therapy

    D. Rational Emotive Behavior Therapy

Answer: D. Rational Emotive Behavior Therapy

The key phrase here is "thinking through irrational thoughts." Reality therapy, Gestalt therapy, and behavior therapy involve therapeutic practices that analyze rational versus irrational thoughts. The correction of these irrational thoughts and the identification of the reality of the moment is the basis of rational-emotive therapy.

41. Questions of freedom, choice and responsibility are addressed in:
    (Average Rigor) (Skill 8.2)

    A. Reality Therapy

    B. Existential Therapy

    C. Behavior Therapy

    D. Person-Centered Therapy

Answer: B. Existential Therapy

Existentialism differs from the psychodynamic and behavior therapies in that it does not rely upon a deterministic view of human nature such as being controlled by irrational actions, past occurrences, and the unconscious.

42. The therapist, in person-centered therapy, should have all the following personality characteristics except:
    (Average Rigor) (Skill 8.2)

    A. Genuineness

    B. Unconditional Positive Regard

    C. Empathic Understanding

    D. Polarized Thinking

Answer: D. Polarized Thinking

The goal of the person-centered therapist is to focus on the client, to make him or her the expert of feelings and events experienced. For a therapist in this or any therapy orientation to have polarized thinking would be detrimental to the process. It would also for bias on the behalf of the therapist and unavailability.

TEACHER CERTIFICATION STUDY GUIDE

43. **The layers of neurosis in Perl's Gestalt theory of neurosis include all of the following except:**
    (Rigorous) (Skill 8.2)

    A. Phobic Layer

    B. Impasse Layer

    C. Meaninglessness layer

    D. Explosive Layer

Answer: C. Meaningless layer

Each layer within Gestalt has a specific meaning or connotation. It would not make sense to have a layer that does not have meaning.

44. **The WDEP model in reality theory includes all the following except:**
    (Rigorous) (Skill 8.2)

    A. Wants

    B. Direction

    C. Evaluation

    D. Planning and Commitment

Answer: B. Direction

The WDEP model is about defining behaviors to target for intervention, setting related goals and executing practices to facilitate behavior change. *Doing*, not direction, is the step in the model when the therapist explores what clients are doing and what direction they taking in their behavior to obtain those wants and needs.

45. In applying counseling theories to specific situations, it is important that the counselor does all of the following except: *(Average Rigor) (Skill 8.3)*

    A. Create a rapport with the student

    B. Pick a theory to use and stick to that theory.

    C. Involve the student in the decision making process

    D. Encourage the student to make his/her own decisions

Answer: B. Pick a theory to apply and stick to that theory

It would be detrimental to the counseling process for a counselor to have such a narrow-minded focus. While the therapist can ascribe to a certain theory, the process needs to be about the client and his/ her needs. It is not uncommon for therapists to utilize multiple theories in order to meet the specific needs of the individual.

46. A concept not used in counseling theory is: *(Rigorous) (Skill 8.3)*

    A. Changing behavior based on present situations

    B. Freud's division of development into five stages

    C. The correction of irrational and illogical thinking

    D. Learning ways to rationalize our behavior

Answer: D. Learning ways to rationalize our behavior

Counseling theory does not teach people how to rationalize behavior or develop other ego-defense mechanisms.

47. **The keys to effective communication include all of the following except:**
    (Rigorous) (Skill 9.1)

    A. Being able to anticipate what the speaker is going to say

    B. Paying attention to nonverbal communication

    C. Asking for clarification

    D. Expressing oneself clearly and directly

Answer: A. Being able to anticipate what the speaker is going to say

Focusing of what you *think* the speaker is going to say interferes with your ability to actually listen to what the speaker is saying.

48. **Elements of good listening skills include all the following except:**
    (Easy) (Skill 9.1)

    A. Involving strong emotions in the process of listening

    B. Being genuinely interested in the speaker

    C. Remembering what has been said

    D. Permitting a speaker to express him/herself fully

Answer: A. Involving strong emotions in the process of listening

The listener is not fully available if his/her emotions are getting in the way; this is called "counter transference." At this point the counselor is projecting their issues into the client's experience, rather than truly listening.

49. Good responding skills include all of the following except:
    (Easy) (Skill 9.1)

    A. Ability to show your feelings without inhibitions

    B. Reflecting back the other person's feelings

    C. Giving constructive feedback

    D. Maintaining eye contact

Answer: A. Ability to show your feelings without inhibitions

Responding should be about the client, not the counselor.

50. Some current sources of professional information for counselors do not include:
    (Easy) (Skill 9.2)

    A. Professional journals

    B. Workshops and conventions

    C. Visitations to other school programs

    D. Teenage magazines

Answer: D. Teenage magazines

Counselors should not rely on popular media as sources of professional information and best practices.

51. Topics for discussion in the initial interview with a student to gain rapport do not include:
    (Rigorous) (Skill 9.3)

    A. Academic progress

    B. Activities in which the student is participating

    C. Difficulties in school adjustment for the entering student

    D. Matters of discipline referral

Answer: D. Matters of discipline referral

The counseling role is not about reprimanding students. Such judgment could be detrimental to building rapport. The initial referral process is sometimes difficult for the counselor if his/her previous interactions with a student have been in consultation with the administration regarding disciplinary issues. It is of paramount importance for the counselor to not include that history or these matters in the initial interview, unless the topic is broached by the student.

52. Ways not to be effective in communicating information to students are:
    (Easy) (Skill 9.3)

    A. Through individual interviews

    B. Through contacting friends and parents

    C. Through home room visitations

    D. Encouraging the student to assess his or her interests and needs

Answer: B. Through contacting friends and parents

Counselor caseloads are often quite large. It is not an effective use of time for counselors to call parents just to inform them of guidance events and deadlines

53. Components of an orientation program should include each of the following except:
(Easy) (Skill 9.4)

   A. Advance notice by mail

   B. Invitations to the entire community

   C. A tour of the facilities

   D. Introduction of counselors and administrators to students and parents with a description of their roles

Answer: B. Invitations to the entire community

Part of advocating for the guidance program and its services is to utilize a variety of methods to both inform and invite.

54. A disadvantage of group counseling is:
(Average Rigor) (Skill 10.1)

   A. The presence of a built in support system

   B. A non-threatening atmosphere

   C. The ability to substitute the group for the real world, permitting the client unlimited time to make adjustments

   D. The counselor can reach more clients

Answer: C. The ability to substitute the group for the real world permitting the client unlimited time to make adjustments

The key words to focus on are "substitute" and "unlimited." The group experience is a one that provides individuals within the group to disclose and challenge problems as well as practice new skills. Due a variety of possible constraints, it should never be assumed that the opportunity of counseling is unlimited. Group counseling creates an alternative environment which clients sometimes begin to associate with to the exclusion of other aspects of their lives, further distorting views of reality.

55. **Limitations of group counseling are all of the following except:**
    (Average Rigor) (Skill 10.1)

    A. There is pressure to accept group values without analyzing them

    B. The counselor has to deal with a diverse population

    C. People sometimes function poorly in groups

    D. Individuals in the group can justify their present status by reinforcement from the group

Answer: B. The counselor has to deal with a diverse population

This answer is vague and is makes an assumption that is too general.

56. **Group dynamics include all the following except:**
    (Rigorous) (Skill 10.2)

    A. A political ideology built on the concept of the organization and management of groups

    B. The employment of specific techniques and concepts to keep the group vitalized.

    C. A branch of knowledge concerned with groups and their interactions, and interactions with other groups and individuals

    D. A description of individual behavior

Answer: D. A way of describing the individual behavior

Focusing on individual behavior misses out on the dynamics of the group experience.

57. Group dynamics is all the following except:
    (Rigorous) (Skill 10.2)

    A. An emphasis on empirical research and theory

    B. A branch of knowledge concerned mainly with the way groups form

    C. The relationships of groups with observable phenomena

    D. The interrelationship of all social science disciplines

Answer: B. A branch of knowledge concerned mainly with the way groups form

This answer seems like it would be appropriate. However, group dynamics is about behavior within the group setting instead of looking at how groups form. Group dynamics must be considered separate from organizational structure. Both impact the functioning of the group, but dynamics will determine client needs and counselor facilitation.

58. The need for specialized programs may be indicated by all of the following except:
    (Rigorous) (Skill 11.1)

    A. Classroom management problems

    B. Targeted grant money

    C. A formal needs assessment

    D. Teacher or counselor observations

Answer: B. Targeted grant money

Classroom problems, teacher or counselor observations and formal needs assessments are all reasons to consider developing a specialized program. The availability of grant money for a special program should not dictate program development; such efforts only make sense if there is also a demonstrated need for the program.

59. **All of the following are good prevention approaches except:**
    (Average Rigor) (Skill 11.2)

    A. Informing parent/guardian(s) about their child's behavior in the school setting

    B. Programs on conflict resolution and communication skills

    C. Anger management groups

    D. Special programs such as the Lunch Bunch

Answer: A. Informing parent/guardian(s) about their child's behavior in the school setting

Telling parent/guardian(s) about what their child is doing in school may or may not be useful to either the parents or the child. It is not a prevention approach, though at times it may be part of a consultation or problem-solving effort.

60. **In using students as a resource in peer leadership the counselor should:**
    (Average Rigor) (Skill 11.2)

    A. Not be present when students are conducting a group

    B. Choose the leaders from potential dropouts

    C. Try not to let the parents know what the process involves

    D. Have the student leaders go through an extensive period of training by a professional

Answer: D. Have the student leaders go through an extensive period of training by a professional

Adequate training is important to the success of any peer leadership program, along with good supervision.

Test I; Part II: Sample Answers for the Constructed Response Assignments

INDIVIDUAL DEVELOPMENT AND LEARNING:
An eight-year-old girl has recently moved to the school district with her family and entered third grade.

- Describe some of the developmental and life issues this student may face.
- Address how these issues may affect her learning process.

Peers are increasingly important to eight year olds, so this girl might be experiencing some difficulty in leaving her previous school and friends and becoming a part of the new peer group. If a family death or other trauma such as job or home loss precipitated the move, there may be complicating factors beyond the usual challenges of a new school setting. How her parents and/or siblings are dealing with the move and the amount of support she has at home will affect how she copes with the transition. It is natural for her to feel some loss as well as uncertainty about the new environment.

Depending on her previous experience as a student and how quickly she is able to become part of the new school environment, this student may or may not have academic troubles. If she is able to focus on learning, she may do well academically even if she is coping with some distress in making friends or settling into the new school. If, after several months, this student continues to have difficulty with learning or achieving her potential (based on prior school records and performance), the counselor should talk with the parents and assess the need for intervention.

COUNSELING AND GUIDANCE:
The school counselor is implementing a peer mediation program for all ninth graders.

- Describe key elements of the program curriculum.
- Address the strategies that will be used to teach this curriculum.

A peer mediation program needs to have a clearly defined process for responding to conflicts between students, including an intake method, a tracking system, a way of assigning peer mediators, an evaluation component, and specific follow-up methods. Prior to starting the program, a comprehensive training is necessary. The training program should include students who wish to become peer mediators as well as faculty and staff who can serve as advisors to the student mediators.

Training for a peer mediation program should include the following topics:

- *core concepts about the process of mediation*
- *diversity awareness*
- *communication skills*
- *how underlying needs drive conflict situations*
- *mediation skills*
- *how to manage a mediation session.*

A variety of teaching strategies are most effective in training peer mediators. Mini-lectures, discussion and case studies are good methods for communicating core concepts about mediation and the process of mediation. Experiential and interactive exercises are best for teaching communication skills and diversity awareness. Practice sessions with role playing and coaching are essential. Student mediators need concrete and specific feedback in these exercises.

TEST II

Test II; Part I: Sample Selected Response Questions

Directions: Read each item and select the best response.

1. Consultation process models include all the following except:
   (Easy) (Skill 12.1)

   A. Doctor/patient model

   B. Friend of the family model

   C. Behavior consultation model

   D. Mental health consultation model

Answer: B. Friend of the family model

There is not an established consultation model based on "friend of the family" and bears no effective application in the process of consultation.

2. The role of consultants in problem solving processes does not include functioning:
   (Average Rigor) (Skill 12.1)

   A. As an advocate

   B. As an expert in a particular area

   C. As a school official

   D. As a process specialist

Answer: C. As a school official

While a school official may be part of the consultation process, they may not be trained to provide a problem-solving process. This would involve a potential conflict of interest.

3. Procedures in the consultation process include all except: (Average Rigor) (Skill 12.1)

   A. Relationship building

   B. Monitoring of the process of behavior change by a neutral party

   C. Evaluation and summarization

   D. Diagnosis of the problem

Answer: B. Monitoring of the process of behavior change by a neutral party

Consultation is an active, dynamic process. Monitoring is not part of the consultation model.

4. The consultation process in the school setting does not include: (Rigorous) (Skill 12.1)

   A. Eliminating the need to counsel students

   B. The meeting of a consultant and a consultee

   C. The solving of a specific problem

   D. Involving consultees (people seeking solutions to student problems)

Answer: A. Eliminating the need to counsel students

Both consultation and counseling serve a vital role in the services the counselor provides. If anything, consultation can further facilitate the need to work with students through the process of counseling.

5. The role the counselor can take in assisting participants in the consultation process does not include:
   (Average Rigor) (Skill 12.2)

   A. Demonstrating classroom behavior management techniques

   B. Describing the nature of the problem

   C. Teaching specific skills

   D. Helping devise strategies to change behaviors

Answer: A Demonstration of classroom behavior management techniques

The role of the counselor is to observe and provide constructive feedback or to provide direct support in identified areas of need. Classroom behavior management is the educator's responsibility and areas of weakness should be addressed by the school administration. The counselor in this situation is present to offer insight to support individual students from a behavioral and social aspect, not to support the classroom educator and his/her class management

6. In the consultation process, communicating student's needs to others does not include:
   (Average Rigor) (Skill 12.2)

   A. Making a judgment by the counselor to others as to what is best for the student

   B. Clarifying the needs of the student with the student

   C. Opening lines of communication between the consultee and the student by having open dialogue

   D. Balancing the needs of the student and the consultee so each can understand the other's position

Answer: A. Making a judgment by the counselor to others as to what is best for the student

Instead of passing judgment, the counselor's role is assist stakeholders in the student's success. The counselor's job is to educate them about the needs of the student based on information gathered from parents and teachers, review the student's academic history, and work with all parties to develop a plan of action

7. **Procedures for successful communication with parent/guardian(s) in the consultation process do not include:**
   (Average Rigor) (Skill 12.2)

   A. Informing parents frequently as to the progress of the resolution of the problem

   B. Using parents as a valuable source of information about the student

   C. Accepting parents ideas for behavior modification

   D. Explaining the problem in simple language as parents are probably unaware of all ramifications

Answer: D. Explaining the problem in simple language as parents are probably unaware of all ramifications

It is appropriate for the counselor to take into the parent's primary language and understanding of certain procedure. This can be established by fact finding and consulting with the student before contacting the parent/guardian(s). However, it is inappropriate to make assumptions about parents' abilities and the level of understanding they bring to any process.

8. **Contributions of parents to the consultation process do not include:**
   (Easy) (Skill 12.2)

   A. Family and medical history

   B. Usually parents do not contribute to the process, as they are uncooperative

   C. Monitoring the child at home

   D. A positive attitude

Answer: B. Usually parents do not contribute to the process, as they are uncooperative.

Regardless of the nature of the information parents provide, inviting the parent to be one of the experts can lead to greater levels of understanding the student's background, strengths, challenges and growth areas. At times, parents' information and suggestions can help create the best possible action plan.

9. **In gathering data for the implementation of a consultation, the counselor should not:**
   (Average Rigor) (Skill 12.2)

   A. Examine the permanent record card for test scores and patterns

   B. Gather medical and discipline history

   C. Consult with an administrator about the student's family history

   D. Talk with the student's teachers to see if they are experiencing the same type of problems

Answer: C. Consult with an administrator about the student's family history

The focus of the consultation is to gain information concerning areas of school functioning that have a direct impact on the student. The student's family history may have an impact and be important, but this information would be learned through meeting with the student and possible the family.

10. **In conducting a consultation follow-up, the counselor should not:**
    (Rigorous) (Skill 12.2)

    A. Gradually decrease participation in the process

    B. Reevaluate after a period of time

    C. Interview the consultee to determine if there is continuing progress

    D. Interview the student and parents in regards to their satisfaction with the consultation

Answer: A. Gradually decrease participation in the process

Follow-up should be ongoing on behalf of the counselor to reevaluate goals and the treatment plan and make adjustments where and when appropriate.

11. **In evaluating the results of consultation, all the following factors should be considered except:**
    (Rigorous) (Skill 12.2)

    A. The feelings of the student's parents as to the success of the process

    B. The report of the consultee as to the problem solving results

    C. An attitude change in the student

    D. Empirical results of an evaluation tool

Answer: D. Empirical results of an evaluation tool

This would serve no effective purpose on the process of consultation. Assessment and monitoring of the evaluation tool is an important step in the process of improving the counseling program, but consideration of the tool should not be considered as a part of each consultation

12. **Family dynamics:**
    (Easy) (Skill 13.1)

    A. Are not relevant to the work of school counselor

    B. Can impact a student's behavior in school

    C. Always play a major role in a student's behavior problems

    D. Rarely affect a student in the school setting

Answer: B. Can impact a student's behavior in school

Family dynamics and conflicts are one of the areas in the student's life that may impact on his or her behavior and functioning in school.

13. Elements of family dynamics include all of the following except: (Rigorous) (Skill 13.1)

    A. Rules and roles within the family

    B. The reinforcement of individual behavior patterns via family interactions

    C. An "identified patient" who serves to divert the family from underlying problems

    D. The parent's childhood background

Answer: D. The parent's childhood background

While a parent's childhood experiences may contribute to who that parent is today and his or her functioning within the family, this background is not fundamentally part of what would be described as "family dynamics." How that parent interested with his or her partner and the children and others in the family would be considered an element of the family dynamics.

14. Components of a program of parental contact do not include: (Average Rigor) (Skill 13.2)

    A. Informing parents of information heard around the school regarding their child

    B. Creating a parent advisory committee

    C. Telephone contact with parents when students are doing well

    D. Small teas and home meetings to inform parents of procedures for their children to maximize education opportunities

Answer: A. Informing parents of information heard around the school regarding their child

The information that counselors share must be founded on well-researched facts. Counselors are charged as both guardians and providers of information. It would unethical to relay such information to a parent or any constituent.

15. **In interactions with school counselors and other school officials, parents and guardians need respect, information and:**
    (Average Rigor) (Skill 3.2)

    A. Positive feedback on their behavior

    B. Confirmation that they are doing a great job with their child

    C. Validation and support

    D. Detailed descriptions of their child's interactions with peers and teachers

Answer: C. Validation and support

Parents and guardians need to be validated and supported in their efforts to help their child. This may or may not include positive feedback per se, or confirmation that they are doing a great job with their child. It is possible to validate and support their efforts without necessarily giving positive feedback or confirmation when the situation doesn't call for such comments. Certainly, if they are doing a good job, then telling them so might be quite appropriate. It is generally not helpful for the counselor to give detailed descriptions of their child's interaction with peers or teachers unless there is an identified problem that needs to be addressed.

16. **In working with parents, a good model to utilize is:**
    (Easy) (Skill 13.2)

    A. Collaborative consultation

    B. Mental health consultation

    C. Family counseling

    D. Advising

Answer: A. Collaborative consultation

Working with parents and guardians in a collaborative manner where each person is bringing relevant and important information to the table is useful. In a school setting, the counselor should not serve as a mental health consultant or family counselor or advisor.

17. **The consultation process with parents does not include**:
    (Rigorous) (Skill 13.2)

    A. Allowing them to vent their frustrations about the school and school officials

    B. Getting to the issue at hand as soon as possible

    C. Clearly delineating the next steps the parent needs to take

    D. Taking care not to make too many suggestions and overwhelm the parent

Answer: C. Clearly delineating the next steps the parent needs to take

Although discussing possible next steps is a significant part of the consultation process with parents, telling them precisely what they need to do is not helpful. This approach conveys an attitude that the "counselor knows best" and discounts the contributions parents and guardians may be able to make in formulating an action plan. It is important to let parents vent their frustrations, as this may be the first time a school official has listened to them. At the same time, getting to the issue at hand is also important.

18. **Data included in the initial referral of a child to a counselor should not include:**
    (Average Rigor) (Skill 13.3)

    A. Unverified illegal behavior

    B. Academic history

    C. Behavior and discipline history

    D. Family history

Answer: A. Unverified illegal behavior

This information has no place in an initial referral to a counselor. If through the process of working with the student there are behaviors of concern (especially when the student is in danger to self or someone else), the counselor should communicate them to the appropriate individuals such as parent/guardian(s), social services and possibly a school administrator.

19. **Procedures for referring a student to an outside agency do not include this information:**
    (Easy) (Skill 13.3)

    A. The counselor has evaluated a need for long-term counseling

    B. The parent feels the child has an emotional problem and asks for an evaluation

    C. The counselor is mandated to report a sexual abuse case

    D. The student doesn't like the counselor

Answer: D. The student doesn't like the counselor

This situation may provide an important learning or growth opportunity for both the student and the counselor if handled in an appropriate, timely and ethical manner. It is not a reason for referral.

20. **School counselors may provide information about which of the following resources for families:**
    (Easy) (Skill 13.3)

    A. Mental health referrals

    B. Food banks and government aid programs

    C. Local support groups

    D. All of the above

Answer: D. All of the above

School counselors are key to providing families with resources about many topics and needs beyond the obvious ones such as financial aid and vocational training.

21. **All but which of the following are important aspects of crisis intervention:** *(Easy) (Skill 14.1)*

    A. Accurate information for those affected by the situation

    B. The latest news reports about the crisis

    C. A school crisis response plan

    D. A systematic way to inform school personnel about the actions to be taken

Answer: B. The latest news reports about the crisis.

Although the media may provide some useful information, for the most part, attending to news reports if not helpful in providing good crisis intervention. Crisis responders need to get information from reliable sources, such as emergency management or law enforcement personnel. Further, the sensationalistic nature of news reports can feed fear and create unnecessary anxiety.

22. **Crisis responders need all of the following except:** *(Easy) (Skill 14.1)*

    A. A chance to debrief and get support from colleagues

    B. Clarity about roles and responsibilities

    C. Mandatory post-trauma counseling

    D. Adequate training and follow-up

Answer: C. Mandatory post-trauma counseling.

Most crisis responders, with adequate training and support, will recover from the effects of providing crisis intervention. In some cases, professional counseling may be helpful or necessary. However, mandating such counseling is inappropriate.

TEACHER CERTIFICATION STUDY GUIDE

23. **An effective advocate does not:**
    (Average Rigor) (Skill 15.1)

    A. Share all information gathered about a particular situation.

    B. Speak up for those who may not have a voice or been heard in the past.

    C. Try to facilitate change

    D. Watch for trends that may indicate underserved populations

Answer: A. Share all information gathered about a particular situation.

During the course of advocacy, people share many personal details with the person helping them. It is not necessary to disclose many of these details in order to effect the needed changes, and in fact is likely to be a betrayal or privacy and confidentiality to do so.

24. **Which of the following is not a form of assessment administered by school counselors:**
    (Easy) (Skill 16.1)

    A. Achievement tests

    B. Intelligence tests

    C. College entrance exams

    D. Performance tests

Answer: B. Intelligence tests

Intelligence tests are generally administered by school psychologists, or psychologists in agencies or the private sector who are trained to do psychological testing.

25. A condition that does not affect testing results is:
    (Rigorous) (Skill 16.1)

    A. The physical and mental condition of the testee

    B. The testing room environment

    C. The colors of the clothes the proctors are wearing

    D. The validity of the test

Answer: C. The colors of the clothes the proctors are wearing

There is no empirical research to date concerning the impact of the colors of the clothes the proctor is wearing on testing results. In addition to the physical and mental condition of the testee, the testing room environment and the preparation of the testee are conditions that can impact testing results as defined by research.

26. All the following are advantages of testing except:
    (Average Rigor) (Skill 16.1)

    A. As a way to get multiple test interpretations

    B. As a way to help students recognize and use the resources they have

    C. As a way to present meaningful information to the student for decision making

    D. As a way to help identify options for the future

Answer: A. As a away to get multiple test interpretations

One of the benefits of testing is to use a standardized process to provide information about the student's performance, access to success and to make recommendations.

27. **Disadvantages of testing are all the following except:**
    (Rigorous) (Skill 16.1)

    A. The possibility of results being used improperly

    B. The possibility of the student misinterpreting the test results

    C. The inherent subjectivity of tests administered for counseling purposes

    D. Using the test to predict future behavior

Answer: D. Using the test to predict future behavior

One of the purposes of testing is to provide a picture of where the student is currently and to anticipate what the student needs to in order to succeed in the future. The process may include identifying barriers to learning, tools needed to increase access to learning and potentially highlighting a process that would be beneficial to the student. However, tests cannot predict future behavior with any certainty.

28. **Informal forms of assessment include all of the following except:**
    (Average Rigor) (Skill 16.1)

    A. Behavioral observation

    B. Learning styles inventories

    C. Sentence completion

    D. Interviewing peers

Answer: D. Interviewing peers

Talking with a student's peers may provide information in a casual context that the school counselor may find useful, but this is not a form of assessment, either formal or informal.

29. In the administration of tests, procedures should include all the following except:
(Rigorous) (Skill 16.2)

    A. Safeguarding the tests

    B. Informing the students of the nature of the test by giving them questions from the test

    C. Guarding the tests in the exam room when students have access to the room

    D. Guarding the tests by not leaving them where students and non-authorized personnel have access

Answer: B. Informing the students of the nature of the test by giving them questions from the test

Since one of the goals of counseling is to build realistic self-concepts, counselors must provide ways to offer useful feedback. Testing can be one of the tools to help students recognize their resources, utilize their strengths and accept their limitations. If students are provided with the test ahead of time, a true picture of the student's abilities and self-concept is not being identified. There is a distinct difference between counseling and instruction; the counselor's job is not to "teach the test" but to inform students of the objectives and testing parameters prior to the event.

TEACHER CERTIFICATION STUDY GUIDE

30. **The inaccuracy of test results caused by chance is called:**
    (Rigorous) (Skill 17.1)

    A. Standardization

    B. Standard Error of Measurement

    C. Standard Score

    D. Derived Score

Answer: B. Standard Error of Measurement

Every test has some element of inaccuracy or unreliability due to chance so this element of the test is taken into consideration when evaluating test results and an allowance is made for this phenomenon. The degree of error is reported in the standard deviation, a specific band of scores. The formula for obtaining the standard error of measurement takes the square root of 1 minus the reliability coefficient.

31. **A statistical concept that measures the relationship between two factors in test validity is:**
    (Rigorous) (Skill 17.1)

    A. Reliability Coefficient

    B. Standard Deviation

    C. Raw Score

    D. Correlation Coefficient

Answer: D. Correlation Coefficient

The reliability coefficient is a statistical concept that measures how reliable the relationship is between two factors in test validity. The standard deviation is the interval of score differences that indicates levels of achievement. The raw score is the basic score usually obtained by counting the number of answers right. It can also be obtained by using the number of wrong answers. The authors of the test can determine any other way to define a raw score.

32. **The specific interval between bands of scores, with each interval indicating a different level of achievement, is called:**
    (Average Rigor) (Skill 17.1)

    A. Reliability Coefficient

    B. Standard Deviation

    C. Raw Score

    D. Correlation Coefficient

Answer: B. Standard Deviation

The standard deviation is a regular (or standard) interval that delineates levels of achievement on normed tests.

33. **If tests need to be interpreted in a group the counselor should not:**
    (Average Rigor) (Skill 18.1)

    A. Announce individual test scores

    B. Explain the norm group to which the students have been compared

    C. Provide for private individual interpretation for students

    D. Explain statistics of the test so students can understand the meaning of their scores

Answer: A. Announce individual test scores

The answers listed in b, c, and d support appropriate components of sharing information in a group setting. Providing information about an individual to a group is not only detrimental to the student-counselor relationship, but it is also unethical.

34. The written report of test results and interpretation should not:
    (Average Rigor) (Skill 18.1)

    A. Be written in understandable language

    B. Always include charts and graphs

    C. Be disseminated on a need to know basis

    D. Be written in the language of testing

Answer: B. Always include charts and graphs

Visual representations within a written report concerning test results are not necessary for understanding them; thus, it is not a critical component of the report.

35. In accurately reporting test results for interpretation by others all the following guidelines should be used except:
    (Rigorous) (Skill 18.1)

    A. A uniform method of recording should be employed

    B. Consistency in language used should be employed

    C. The purpose, limitations, and the validity of the test should be stated

    D. The receiver of the results should be required to contact the counselor in order to receive the counselor's candid opinion

Answer: D. The receiver of the results should be required to contact the counselor in order to receive the counselor's candid opinion

While it is not in appropriate to contact the counselor for further explanation or clarification of test results, seeking a "candid opinion" can misconstrue or confound the nature of the results.

36. **In interpreting test results the counselor should not:**
    (Average Rigor) (Skill 18.2)

    A. Relate the results to the goals that had previously been determined

    B. Provide for individual interpretation

    C. Wait to interpret the tests when the student is scheduling the following year's courses

    D. Give the student input into the interpretation of the test results

Answer: C. Wait to interpret the tests when the student is scheduling the following year's courses

The work of a school counselor is to help the student maximize their performance. If a counselor delays in providing information to a student, it could contribute to student failure instead of success.

37. **In interpreting test results to other professionals and parents, the counselor does not always have to:**
    (Average Rigor) (Skill 18.2)

    A. Be thoroughly familiar with the test

    B. Let other staff members see the results of the test

    C. Notify the student that the counselor will be sharing the results with their parent/guardian(s)

    D. Work with the parents in a counseling relationship to help them understand their child's abilities

Answer: B. Let other staff members see the results of the test

Sharing test results with other staff should first be discussed with the student and the student's parents. Depending on the nature of the test, other personnel often do not need to know the results and it best to keep it confidential. The confidential nature of the counseling role demands caution in the dissemination of information concerning students.

38. **In interpreting testing data from other professionals and testing firms, the counselor should do all the following except:**
    (Average Rigor) (Skill 18.2)

    A. Understand the material in the report

    B. Go right to the summary and not worry about the technical aspects of the report

    C. Contact the writer of the report for clarification if needed

    D. Refer to the testing manual for clarification if needed

Answer: B. Go right to the summary and not worry about the technical aspects of the report

It is important that the counselor provide an explanation that honors the purpose and motivation for the testing. Looking at the technical aspects of the report may offer important information to this end.

39. **A good guidance program does not include:**
    (Easy) (Skill 19.1)

    A. A pay scale for counselors higher than other staff members in order to attract quality people

    B. An adequate budget to supply the basic tools needed for the program

    C. Trained, certified, professional counselors

    D. A mission statement

Answer: A. A pay scale for counselors higher than other staff members in order to attract quality people

Professionally and ethically speaking, pay scale should not be a factor in the quality of a guidance program.

40. The goals of the guidance program should not include:
    (Rigorous) (Skill 19.1)

    A. Acquisition of academic skills by the student population commensurate with their abilities

    B. Acquisition of personal insights by students

    C. Learned ability to make intelligent choices

    D. Selection of a lifetime career

Answer: D. Selection of a lifetime career

Counselors can and should provide events, materials and discussions about the role of career and occupation with students, teachers, parents, administrators and members of the surrounding community. A goal of the counseling program should be to facilitate career exploration. In the process of such structured and carefully planned and executed career guidance a student may feel motivated to pursue a certain career, but it is not a criterion of an effective guidance program.

41. Techniques to let the community know what is happening in guidance do not include:
    (Easy) (Skill 19.1)

    A. A guidance newsletter

    B. A letter to the editor regarding the school board cutting guidance staff

    C. Speaking about the guidance program to local civic organizations

    D. Involving community leaders as members of an advisory board

Answer: B. A letter to the editor regarding the school board cutting guidance staff

Such a letter would not be an effective way to let the community know about the guidance department, nor would it be a collaborative or positive action to take in general.

42. **The type of research in which counselors would not engage is:**
    (Rigorous) (Skill 19.2)

    A. Historical

    B. Single subject experimental

    C. Assessment and evaluation

    D. Qualitative

Answer: B. Single subject experimental

Single subject experimental research focuses on the individual and not on the results of group experimentation. It is used to test hypotheses of the effect of a particular treatment on one or more behaviors or phenomena. This type of research would not help a counselor gain the tools necessary to be able to be effective in his or her work with students.

43. **The purpose of research in which a working counselor would not engage is:**
    (Average Rigor) (Skill 19.2)

    A. Basic research to obtain knowledge without the need for practical application

    B. Applied research to obtain general ways to improve education

    C. To develop a theory for creating generalizations

    D. Action research to immediately apply results to a specific problem

Answer: C. To develop a theory for creating generalizations

This answer is self-explanatory. It would be little to no use for a school counselor to formulate a theory for the purpose of creating generalizations.

44. **The research evaluation stages of the CIPP model do not include:**
    (Rigorous) (Skill 19.2)

    A. Context evaluation

    B. Process evaluation

    C. Input evaluation

    D. Program evaluation

Answer: D. Program evaluation

The CIPP (Context, Input, Process, Product) Model has four stages: Context evaluation, input evaluation, process evaluation, and product evaluation.

45. **Formative evaluation does not involve:**
    (Rigorous) (Skill 19.3)

    A. Collection of data in the developmental stage of research

    B. Collection of data in the implementation stage of research

    C. Collection of data after a program has been in place a period of time

    D. Collection of data when the research is in the operational stage

Answer: C. Collection of data after a program has been in place a period of time

This type of evaluation involves the collection of data while a program is in the developmental, implementation, and the operational stage

TEACHER CERTIFICATION STUDY GUIDE

46. In conducting a program needs assessment the following individuals should be included:
    (Rigorous) (Skill 19.3)

    A. Students only

    B. Administrators only

    C. People in the community who have no students in school

    D. The community, students, staff, administrators, and parents

Answer: D. The community, students, staff, administrators, and parents

It is imperative that all members of the school community including parents are given the opportunity to provide feedback about guidance counseling services; this is the only way in which counselors will generate a clear picture of the needs of the community. The integration of all stakeholders is key to the success of any needs assessment.

47. The determining factors of the worth of a program do not include:
    (Rigorous) (Skill 19.4)

    A. How well the program fits preconceived ideas of intended outcomes

    B. Statistical significance

    C. Interpretation of the meaning of the results

    D. The practicality of implementing the program for every day use

Answer: A. How well the program fits preconceived ideas of intended outcomes

Evaluative data and the practicality of implementing a program for everyday use should guide the determination of the value of a program. Fitting into preconceived goals is not necessarily useful in assessing a program's worth.

48. **Program objectives are:**
    (Rigorous) (Skill 19.4)

    A. Created to fit the outcomes of the research

    B. Readjusted as the need arises

    C. Determined after the program has been operational for a period of time

    D. Formulated before the research is instituted

Answer: D. Formulated before the research is instituted

An effective guidance program needs to be based on research in order to be sound in its validity.

49. **In evaluating a newly created program, the counselor should:**
    (Rigorous) (Skill 19.4)

    A. Ask the guidance staff if they think the program is working

    B. Ask students informally what they think of the program

    C. Conduct an extensive evaluation of all involved that includes surveys, questionnaires, and observations

    D. After three months, evaluate the program and make a recommendation

Answer: C. Conduct an extensive evaluation of all involved that includes surveys, questionnaires, and observations

Using formal and organized methods of assessment provides structure to the information-gathering process as well as makes it easier to compile statistical information.

50. Before introducing new and innovative programs to the guidance curriculum the counselor should first:
    (Rigorous) (Skill 19.4)

    A. Ask the administration for a budget for the program

    B. Conduct a needs assessment survey

    C. Arrange for a pilot program

    D. Contact Board of Education members to get them to agree on the implementation of the program

Answer: B. Conduct a needs assessment survey

Just because a program is innovative and has a lot to offer does not mean it will meet the needs of the respective school community. It is critical for school counselors to have a pulse on the needs of the community they serve. It is imperative that the school counselor develops a program improvement model that clearly outlines action steps for the creation, monitoring, and support of any and all programs that are utilized.

51. Guidelines for ethical behavior written in the ACA Code of Ethics and Standards of Practice include all of the following areas except:
    (Rigorous) (Skill 20.1)

    A. Penalties for specific ethical violations

    B. Confidentiality

    C. Resolving of ethical issues

    D. Relationships with other professionals

Answer: A. Penalties for specific ethical violations

The key word to focus on is "guidelines." There are too many factors involved to have potential penalties discussed in the body of this work.

52. The purpose of the National Board of Certified Counselors (NBCC) is to:
    (Average Rigor) (Skill 20.1)

    A. Issue practice credentials

    B. Resolve ethical issues

    C. Certify professionals to assure a high level of competence

    D. Bargain for higher salaries for guidance professionals

Answer: C. Certify professionals to assure a high level of competence

It is not possible to guarantee the level of competence of counselors.

53. When an ethical issue arises in a counselor's practice the counselor should:
    (Average Rigor) (Skill 20.1)

    A. Refer to the ACA code of Ethics

    B. Decide what to do immediately so the problem will not linger

    C. Ask the client what to do

    D. Consult with the Board of Education

Answer: A. Refer to the ACA Code of Ethics

54. Continuing professional development is important for school counselors for all of the following reasons except:
    (Easy) (Skill 20.2)

    A. To keep abreast of changes in professional practices and standards

    B. To utilize all available monies in the budge for staff development

    C. To be refreshed and renewed as a professional

    D. To further develop counseling skills

Answer: B. To utilize all available monies in the budget for staff development

Continuing education and development is geared to support and expand the school counselor's capacity to function well. In many cases, the counselor may spend his or her own money to get appropriate training or learn new skills.

55. Parents, guardians, and students have a right to all the following records except:
    (Rigorous) (Skill 21.1)

    A. Copies of all records relating to the student

    B. Copies of all student records containing comparisons of the student with other students

    C. All the student's records maintained by public institutions

    D. A list of all types of records directly related to the student

Answer: B. Copies of all student records containing comparisons of the student with other students

Parents and eligible students only have access to their specific child's records. It would be a violation of another student's rights to have his/her information viewed by an undesignated person. Confidentiality and parent/student rights are a paramount concern for the school counselor. His/her success and the quality of the program depend on such confidentiality.

56. The rights of parents, students, and guardians does not include:
    (Average Rigor) (Skill 21.1)

    A. Right of access

    B. Right of privacy

    C. Right to challenge and a hearing

    D. Right to alter the written record if they feel it is not true

Answer: D. Right to alter the written record if they feel it is not true

Parents may advocate for personal information to be corrected when they have the appropriate documentation to support the change. However, parents may not request the student's academic record be altered in any way.

57. Who are not the people limited to a "need to know" basis with regard to student assessment data:
    (Average Rigor) (Skill 21.1)

    A. The newspapers

    B. School personnel

    C. The counselor, school psychologist, school social worker and principal

    D. Attorneys

Answer: C. The counselor, school psychologist, school social worker and principal

The counselor, school psychologist, school social worker and the principal use student data to identity existing patterns, strengths, growth areas and action oriented solutions to help maximize student performance and achievement.

58. Written permission must be obtained to release assessment data from:
    (Average Rigor) (Skill 21.1)

    A. The counselor

    B. The student over 18 or the student's parent or guardian

    C. The Board of Education

    D. The teacher who generated the assessment data

Answer: B. The student over 18 or the student's parent or guardian

Since counseling is a confidential relationship, the counselor should obtain permission from the student to release any information given in confidence. However, if the student is under 18, even if the information is gathered in reference to services provided due to a disability (i.e. IDEA qualifications), written permission needs to be procured from the parent or legal guardian.

59. The intent of the Individuals with Disabilities Act of 1975 was all of the following except:
    (Rigorous) (Skill 21.2)

    A. To give children with disabilities special services to make up for past discriminations

    B. To give children with disabilities a free and appropriate education

    C. To provide for the needs of children with disabilities

    D. To prevent discrimination against children with disabilities

Answer: A. To give children with disabilities special services to make up for past discriminations

IDEA is about providing students equal access to education. No one student should have more access to education services due to past issues of discrimination.

60. School counselors are required to report suspected child abuse and neglect by all of the following people except:
 (Rigorous) (Skill 21.3)

   A. A parent or guardian

   B. Someone living in the child's home

   C. The child's caregiver

   D. A grandparent

Answer: D. A grandparent

Child abuse by a grandparent is not required to be reported to Child Protective Services unless the grandparent is living in the child's home (Option B).

Test II; Part II: Sample Answers for the Constructed Response Assignments

CONSULTATION AND COLLABORATION:
A well-loved custodian at the middle school died suddenly over the weekend. The school principal has asked the school counselor to help the students and families cope with this loss.

- Describe what strategies the counselor might employ.
- Discuss the value of these strategies.

The school counselor's first task is to consult the school crisis plan and follow the guidelines outlined there. Initial strategies might include launching a phone chain to notify faculty and staff, and discussing with the crisis team leader what tasks need to be addressed immediately. Subsequent strategies may include determining how students will be informed of the death, preparing a letter to be sent home to parents and guardians, and setting up a room for students to come to if they are experiencing difficulty or need to talk. Links with community agencies and programs may also need to be made.

The importance of the above strategies is several. All school response efforts need to be coordinated. Collaboration is key. A specific plan about interventions is also essential, so the school day can proceed as normally as possible while still providing the necessary support. All members of the school community need accurate information about the situation, including funeral and viewing arrangements, as well as any memorial the school may be doing. This can help everyone feel a part of things; a shared experience allows for healing and decreases the likelihood of adverse reactions.

PROFESSIONAL IDENTITY AND PRACTICE:
The grandparent of a high school senior contacts the school counselor about the senior's recent performance test results and offers information about the student.

- Describe the circumstances under which the counselor may or may not discuss the test results with the grandparent.
- Discuss what other steps the counselor needs to take regarding disclosure and notification as a result of contact with the grandparent.

A student's test results may not be shared with anyone other than the student and his parents or legal guardians. If the grandparent is a legal guardian, then the counselor may discuss the test scores. Otherwise, the counselor needs to let the grandparent know that this information is confidential and can only be shared with the permission of the student and the parents. If the student is 18 years of age, he may give permission for the counselor to disclose his test results without parental consent. The counselor can thank the grandparent for sharing the information about the student, and let the grandparent know that she will be letting the student and parents know that the grandparent called and is concerned.

*If the grandparent **is** the student's legal guardian, then it is appropriate for the counselor to simply let the student know that his grandparent called. The counselor can tell the student briefly what was shared and ask any follow-up questions regarding the information from the grandparent if there are any concerning issues. If the grandparent **is not** the legal guardian, the counselor needs to let the student and the parents know she has been contacted by the grandparent. She can give a brief summary of the conversation. The goals are to keep everyone informed, so there is no confusion about what has transpired, and to maintain the trusting relationships with the student and the parents.*

www.ingramcontent.com/pod-product-compliance
Lightning Source LLC
Chambersburg PA
CBHW080537300426